DON JUAN

ALSO BY RICHARD WILBUR

JEAN BAPTISTE POQUELIN DE

Molière

DON JUAN

COMEDY IN FIVE ACTS, 1665

TRANSLATED INTO ENGLISH BY
RICHARD WILBUR

A HARVEST BOOK
HARCOURT, INC.
SAN DIEGO   NEW YORK   LONDON

Library of Congress Cataloging-in-Publication Data
Molière, 1622–1673
[Don Juan. English]
Don Juan: comedy in five acts, 1665/Jean Baptiste Poquelin de Molière; translated into English by Richard Wilbur.
p. cm.—(A Harvest book)
ISBN 0-15-601310-X
1. Don Juan (Legendary character)—Drama.   I. Wilbur, Richard, 1921– II. Title.
PQ1831 .A48 2001
842'.4—dc21   00-040749

Printed in the United States of America

DOM 14 13 12 11 10 9 8 7 6 5

for my son Nathan

INTRODUCTION

Don Juan, Molière's first full-scale comedy in prose, appropriated a tale which, first told by the Spanish dramatist Tirso de Molina in his *El Burlador de Sevilla* (1630), had been reworked at mid-century for the Italian theatre of Cicignini and Giliberto, and adapted to the conventions of French tragicomedy by the playwrights Dorimon and Villiers. From the box-office point of view, any treatment of the familiar plot was likely to succeed, since it offered sensational misbehavior, the supernatural, and a chance for bang-up special effects. It may be, as some have conjectured, that Molière was partially drawn to retell the Don Juan story—the story of an impious man's punishment—in the hope of placating the religious militants who had forced *Tartuffe* off the boards in 1664. If that was any part of his motivation, Molière miscalculated, for when *Don Juan* opened at the Palais-Royal in February of the next year, a storm of pious censure forced the author to make cuts after the first performance and to close the play—despite good business—after the fifteenth. Molière never published or revived the work, and after his death it was effectively replaced by Thomas Corneille's inoffensive verse adaptation, which Molière's widow had commissioned and which played in French theatres for almost two centuries. Not until 1813 was a full and restored text of Molière's *Don Juan* published in France; not until 1847 did the play enter the repertoire of the Comédie Française.

In the twentieth century, however, this long-suppressed play came to enjoy brilliant productions in France, and so much attention from critics and scholars everywhere that Jacques Guicharnaud, in a 1964 essay on Molière, could call *Don Juan* "the center of attention among all the works." There are many cultural factors which might account for the play's changed fortunes, and for our present receptivity to it, but certainly this is true: that the pervasive ambiguity of the work, which offended the devout of Molière's day, is for us a source of richness and nuance.

Don Juan is not a classically constructed comedy but a loose, two-day sequence of episodes which rambles through the vaguest of Sicilies. It is somewhat held together, in the plot sense, by the continuing stories of the Commander and of Elvira and her brothers, as well as by the theme of damnation, which is present from the first scene onward. But its main coherence lies in a many-angled portrayal, in varying circumstances and social milieux, of the title character, who with his servant Sganarelle is centrally present in all but two scenes. That this character will fulfill his legend by ending in hellfire, and that he will deserve that fate, one assumes from the start; yet Molière is at pains to create a complex Don Juan with whom we can to some extent sympathize, and in whom we can see certain attractive qualities. To this end he eliminates the crudely violent deeds—rape, father-beating, and the like—which earlier Don Juans had performed, soft-pedals the Commander's killing by putting it into the past, and permits his hero little in the way of successful on-stage wickedness: the Don's amatory initiatives are frustrated by shipwreck or interruption, the Poor Man stands up to him, and only M. Dimanche is fully victimized. On the positive side, Molière's Don Juan is repeatedly shown to be a courageous, witty, eloquent, and handsome young man, whose behavior can appear to embody a brave independence of every code and orthodoxy. That appearance is made the more possible by the fact that all the conventions, as advocated or embodied in the play, give signs of hollowness or fragility.

There being no *raisonneur* on hand, the cause of religion is argued in muddled commonplaces by the foolish Sganarelle, whose want of true piety is proven when he urges the Poor Man to blaspheme. Though Elvira can be moving and genuine in her fervor for the hero, she damages the idea of courtly love when she reproaches the Don for not telling her elegant lies; and the religious exaltation of her second appearance has a theatrical quality which cannot be sustained, as she helplessly modulates toward a restatement of her passion. The Poor Man, in Act Three, is a fine example of spiritual integrity, yet it may be (as some contend) that we would think even better of him if he did not take money for his prayers. Later in the same act, Molière presents the gentleman's code of honor in a dubious light, both because of Don Carlos's humane reservations about it, and be-

cause of his brother's feral eagerness to enforce it. Don Luis's reproaches in Act Four, which nobly assert the idea that high rank
is nothing without virtue, are somewhat undermined by the re-
flection that he has long been using his influence to effect a
cover-up of his son's criminal career. The shakiness of codes and
conventions in *Don Juan*'s world, and a measure of inauthentic-
ity in all their representatives, enable the Don to hear people
with unnerving silence, to dismiss Sganarelle's arguments with
curt derision, to respond to the tirades of Elvira or Don Luis
with deflating mock-politeness, and in every case to direct the
play's laughter against the other characters.

Because the laugh is never on Don Juan, some readers of the
play have identified with him, seeing him as the free-spirited,
self-determining hero of an "anti-Establishment" satire. Doubtless such readers would also distort *The Misanthrope* (which
Molière was working on at the time of *Don Juan*'s composition),
taking the self-deceived, self-dramatizing, and antisocial Alceste
to be a fearless critic of conventional insincerities. Such misread-
ings are not utterly wrong, but they are oversimple, anachronis-
tic, and a little humorless. We find a truer, subtler sense of *Don
Juan* in this sentence of Irving Singer's: "The play—which
everyone admits to be a difficult one—achieves its unique ambiguity by using Don Juan to reveal the hypocrisy of everyone else
at the same time as they show him to be the monster that he is."

Though he kills no one before our eyes, and though we do not
witness what Don Luis calls "the multitude of his misdeeds," the
young nobleman whom Molière shows us is indeed a monster.
He is a serial lover who, by his own account, is repeatedly "ravished" by beauty, and who, having suffered that "sweet violence," rallies his forces and pursues the woman of the moment
until she physically surrenders. Thereafter, he is done with her
and ready for another "conquest." To the adolescent fantast in us
all, such a program is appealing, yet what it argues is a desperate
deficiency—a brutish inability to treat people as persons, an in-
capacity for the creative act of loving. Don Juan can be bitterly
aware of what he lacks, and when, toward the end of Act One,
Scene Two, he expresses envy of two happy lovers, and proposes
to "mar their felicity" by piratical violence, he sounds like Milton's

Satan first beholding Adam and Eve "Imparadised in one another's arms." Because he descends from a chivalrous élite, Don Juan seeks to dignify his amours by likening them to military campaigns; and in fact his martial metaphors *are* appropriate to his conduct, in love or out. Whatever pleasure the Don may gain from beauty, or from successive marriage beds, the thing that really matters to him is victory; for him, every human encounter is a battle that he must win. He must intimidate Pierrot, and hoodwink the peasant girls Charlotte and Mathurine, and frustrate M. Dimanche with false courtesies; and when the Poor Man will not be bribed, the Don must hasten to keep the upper hand by giving him the gold piece anyway. The one restraint upon Don Juan, as we learn in the Cornelian situations of Act Three, is the gentleman's code of honor, which he observes not because he believes in it but because to be seen as a gentleman is an essential underpinning for his pride.

What kind of pride is it that one sees in Don Juan? It is an unbounded pride, which longs for "still more worlds" in which to have its way; at the same time, it is an anxious, driven pride which must bolster itself by incessant acts of domination, and in its uneasy self-absorption can spare no sympathy or respect for humankind. It is not the pride of a free man, but of one who is the slave of his fears and compulsions. For Don Juan the *conquistador*, other people are either antagonists or victims; they are also, despite the Don's pretensions to independence, an audience before whom he plays, and on whose witness to his magnetic singularity he depends. His reformation, he says to Don Luis in Act Five, "will astound the world," and it has always been his need to hold the world's attention. This cold, strange young man, who must at every moment dazzle and prevail, can afford only one intimate or confidant in all creation—his valet and jester Sganarelle. Though Sganarelle ultimately resists Don Juan, and at the close of the play mourns not his master but his unpaid wages, it is easy to see how well he answers the Don's need to be safely open with someone. As a servant, Sganarelle is readily dominated; his speeches can be heard with amused contempt, and he can at any moment be bullied into silence. He is also a captive audience of one, before whom the hero struts and defines himself, and despite his timorous moralism he frequently—as in his treatment of M. Dimanche—pays Don Juan the tribute of imitation.

When Don Juan announces to Sganarelle, in Act Five, his intention to become a hypocrite, it would be a mistake to see it as the capitulation of a once-bold social rebel. As W. G. Moore has said, it will not do to view Don Juan as "a prophet of secularism" and the Enlightenment, and if we want to discover his type in history we should think instead of the arrogant and wilful feudal nobility whose power Louis XIV had tamed. Some critics, dissatisfied with the Don's decision, have accused Molière of twisting the plot in order to motivate a long speech unfavorable to that "cabal of the pious" which had been persecuting him. No doubt that is part of the answer; however, it seems to me that the Don's resort to dissimulation is a sufficiently logical development. His affairs have come to a crisis. He needs to appease his irate father, whose help and protection are vital to him, and his pursuit by Elvira's brothers has made him aware that he needs allies against those he has wronged. In resolving to play the part of reformed sinner, he sacrifices one aspect of himself—the image of the swaggering young lord who is a law unto himself. But there is another side of his prideful character—his scorn for the truth and his relish for deception—of which hypocrisy could be the ultimate expression. There are, in Act Five, two kinds of hypocritical utterance by Don Juan: his words to his father are plain bamboozlement, but what he says to Don Carlos is a teasing, transparent lie (like his "utterly sincere" address to Elvira in Act One) which the hearer is not in a position to dismiss, and which represents falsehood at its most contemptuous.

When I said earlier that the laugh is never on Don Juan, I was thinking of the audible laughter of a theatre audience. This play also provokes a great deal of inward amusement, even in scenes of a poignant or "tragic" character, and that is what makes it possible for so heterogeneous a work to give a final impression of comic unity. Don Juan is extremely attentive in all situations, because of his compulsion to win, but he can at the same time be unshakably resistant and indifferent. That is the case in the play's third scene, when he finds himself overtaken by Elvira, the wife whom he has deserted. His first reaction is not to look at her or acknowledge her presence. His second response is a brief and wonderfully inadequate expression of surprise. When Elvira then passionately denounces his treachery, and challenges him to account for it, he tells her with Brummellian superciliousness that his valet will explain his departure. Finding that explanation unintelligible, Elvira scaldingly reproaches the Don for lacking a courtier's eloquent excuses, and to that he responds with mocking dishonesty and a preemptive piety, claiming to have left her for reasons of conscience. Her parting tirade, in which she proclaims that Heaven will avenge her, is punctuated by impious banter between Don Juan and Sganarelle, and is immediately followed by the Don's saying, "Now then, let's go ahead with our [next] amorous enterprise." Though Elvira's situation deserves our sympathy, and though her stormy speeches are moving and just, the scene is comic or absurd throughout because in the emotional sense Don Juan hears nothing, and replies only with cold parrying, mockery, and obfuscation. H. Gaston Hall finds a similar comedy of noncommunication in the first scene (Act Four, Scene Four) between Don Luis and his son: "The two characters are in a comic situation because they speak and understand in two incompatible planes." When Don Juan, in Act Three, bids Sganarelle invite the Commander's statue to dinner, the valet replies, "I'd be crazy if I went and talked to a statue." There is a similar craziness or absurdity in any character's trying to have a heart-to-heart talk with Don Juan, who is at least as stony as the Commander.

Is Don Juan himself a comic figure? Yes. It may be that his disbelief in Heaven is a deficiency, like his inability to love a woman, but it comes across as aggressive and cocksure, and that makes him comic in the circumstances of this play—just as it was comic for certain English scientists, presented in 1798 with the skin of a duck-billed platypus, to declare it a hoax because it did not fit into their rigid scheme of Nature. If we are not to be provincially contemporary, we must—as Gaston Hall says—accept the supernatural in *Don Juan* as we accept the ghost in *Hamlet* or the witches in *Macbeth*. If we do, Hall goes on to say, we may then see "that in refusing to heed the warnings of Sganarelle, of Don Luis, and of Doña Elvira, as in refusing to accept the *evidence* of the miracle wrought in the Statue, Don Juan is comic in exactly the same ways as Orgon when he refuses to consider the evidence gathered against Tartuffe." Don Juan is by far the cleverest person in the play which bears his name, and that makes it all the more ridiculous that he should be stupid about the ultimate question of God's existence. To quote Dr. Hall a final time, "Is there not something comic about a man borne off by a force in which he refused to believe?"

Don Juan is not in verse, like the other Molière plays I have translated, but its prose presents some formal challenges which I hope to have met. There are times when Molière's prose dialogue slips into the rhythms of the alexandrine, and the translation should, at such moments, do something similar without overdoing it. There are in the play a great many styles of speaking to be duplicated, from the lofty periods of Don Luis to the mercantile servility of M. Dimanche, and the hero and his valet have several voices each; indeed, in the very first moments of the play we find Sganarelle assuming a pseudosophisticated tone, and seeking to impress a fellow servant with a fatuous digression on snuff. The chief problem of diction for the translator of *Don Juan* is, of course, how to render the speech of Pierrot, Charlotte, and Mathurine in Act Two. Though those characters are supposedly Sicilian peasants, they are altogether French; Molière has given them French names and has had them speak in a patois of the Paris region which, though incidentally amusing, would have been entirely intelligible to his audience. It seemed to me that the peasants should also be easy to understand in English, and so I have avoided the quaint densities of dialect, settling instead for some ordinary bad grammar and for the familiar locutions of rural New England.

When in doubt, I have sometimes consulted earlier translations by Wall, Gravely, Wood, Frame, or Porter, and am grateful for their help. I thank my wife for her patient criticism, and my friends William Jay Smith and Sonja Haussmann Smith for their great kindness in looking over the finished text.

R. W.
Cummington, 1997

DON JUAN

CHARACTERS

DON JUAN—son of Don Luis

SGANARELLE—Don Juan's valet

ELVIRA—wife of Don Juan

GUSMAN—squire to Elvira

DON CARLOS—Elvira's brother

DON ALONSO—Elvira's brother

DON LUIS—father of Don Juan

A POOR MAN

CHARLOTTE—a peasant girl

MATHURINE—a peasant girl

PIERROT—a peasant

THE STATUE OF THE COMMANDER

LA VIOLETTE—servant to Don Juan

RAGOTIN—servant to Don Juan

MONSIEUR DIMANCHE—a merchant

LA RAMÉE—a roughneck

ATTENDANTS on Don Carlos and Don Alonso

A SPECTRE

The action takes place in Sicily.

3

ACT ONE

SCENE ONE

SGANARELLE, GUSMAN
A palace or palatial public building.

SGANARELLE *(With a snuff-box in his hand.)*

Whatever Aristotle and the other old philosophers may say, there's nothing so fine as snuff. All the best people are devoted to it, and anyone who lives without snuff doesn't deserve to live. Not only does it purge and stimulate the brain, it also schools the soul in goodness, and one learns in using it how to be a true gentleman. You've noticed, I'm sure, how whenever a man takes a pinch of snuff, he becomes gracious and benevolent toward everybody, and delights in offering his snuff-box right and left, wherever he happens to be. He doesn't wait to be asked, but antici-pates the unspoken desires of others—so great is the gen-erosity which snuff inspires in all who take it. But enough of that subject; let's go back a bit to what we were dis-cussing. So then, my dear Gusman, your mistress Doña Elvira was surprised by our sudden departure, and has come galloping after us. Her heart, you say, is so deeply enamored of my master that she couldn't live unless she followed him here. Now, just between us, would you like to hear what I think about these developments? I fear that her love will be ill-rewarded, that her trip to this city will be fruitless, and that you'd have done better to stay at home.

[*Act One • Scene One*]

GUSMAN

Pray, why do you say that? What leads you, Sganarelle, to make so grim a prediction? Has your master confided in you about this business? Has he told you of some displeasure with us which caused him to leave?

SGANARELLE

Nothing of the sort. But, judging by certain signs, I know pretty well how things are likely to go. Though he hasn't yet told me anything, I'd almost wager that the affair will end as I said. I could be mistaken, of course; but long experience has given me some insight in these matters.

GUSMAN

What! Do you mean to say that Don Juan's unexpected departure was an act of infidelity? Could he so disdain the chaste love of Doña Elvira?

SGANARELLE

No, no, it's just that he's still young, and can't yet bring himself...

GUSMAN

Could a man of his rank behave so basely?

SGANARELLE

Ah yes, his rank! What a quaint idea! As if his rank could deter him from doing what he likes!

[*Act One • Scene One*]

GUSMAN

But the man is bound by the sacred ties of marriage!

SGANARELLE

Ah, my poor Gusman, you don't begin to know, believe me, what sort of man Don Juan is.

GUSMAN

It's true indeed that I don't know the man, if he can break faith with us in such a way. I don't understand how, after so many professions of love and importunate desire, so many sighs, promises, and tears, so many ardent letters, so many fervent speeches and reiterated vows, so many wild and passionate actions as well, wherein he went so far as to force the gates of a holy convent to gain possession of Doña Elvira—I don't understand, I repeat, how after all that he could have the gall to go back on his word.

SGANARELLE

As for me, I've no trouble understanding it; and if you knew his shifty character you'd see that such behavior comes natural to him. I'm not saying that his feelings toward Doña Elvira have altered—I can't as yet be sure about that: as you know, he had me leave town ahead of him, and since his arrival here he's told me nothing. But, just to prepare you for the worst, I tell you *inter nos* that the person you've known as Don Juan, my master, is the greatest scoundrel who ever walked the earth, a mad dog, a demon, a Turk, a heretic who doesn't believe in Heaven, or Hell, or werewolves even. He lives like a brute

beast, an Epicurean swine, an absolute Sardanapalus, clos-
ing his ears to all reproaches and treating all our noblest
credences as nonsense. You mention that he has married
your mistress; believe you me, he'd have done more than
that if necessary. For the sake of his passion, he'd have
married you too, and her dog and her cat to boot. Getting
married means nothing to him; it's simply his technique
for ensnaring beautiful women, and he'll marry anything.
A noble lady, a young woman of quality, a merchant's
daughter, a peasant wench—there's nothing narrow
about his tastes; and if I told you the names of all the
women he's married in one place or another, it would take
from now until sundown. You stand there pale and aston-
ished at what I've said; but what you've heard was the
merest sketch of the subject, and a true portrait would
need many more strokes of the brush. Suffice it to say
that the wrath of Heaven hangs over him every day, that
I'd be safer in the Devil's employ than in his, and that he
involves me in so many enormities that I wish he were
already in you-know-where. But a great lord who's a
wicked man is a frightening thing; I must be loyal to him,
whether I like it or not. I serve him not from zeal but
from fear, which makes me hide my true feelings and re-
duces me, very often, to applauding what my soul detests.
But here he comes now, strolling through the halls of this
palazzo; we must separate. Bear this in mind, however:
I've confided in you very frankly, and my words have
spilled out in an unguarded fashion; but if anything I've
said should come to his ears, I shall swear up and down
that you're a liar.

SCENE TWO

DON JUAN

With whom were you speaking, just now? I'd say that he looks much like the good Gusman, Doña Elvira's servant.

SGANARELLE

The resemblance could not be closer.

DON JUAN

What? Then it's he?

SGANARELLE

The same.

DON JUAN

And since when has he been in this town?

SGANARELLE

Since yesterday evening.

[*Act One • Scene Two*]

DON JUAN

And what business brings him here?

SGANARELLE

I think you can surmise what's on his mind.

DON JUAN

Our departure, no doubt?

SGANARELLE

The old fellow is greatly grieved by it, and was asking me to explain your motives.

DON JUAN

And what did you tell him?

SGANARELLE

That you hadn't informed me of them.

DON JUAN

But come now, what's your opinion about this turn of events? What do you suppose is going on?

SGANARELLE

What do I think? I think—no offense intended—that you've got some new beloved on the brain.

DON JUAN

That's what you think?

SGANARELLE

Yes.

DON JUAN

My word, you're quite right! I must own that another charmer has banished Elvira from my thoughts.

SGANARELLE

Of course, what else? I know my Don Juan inside and out, and I know that your heart is the most restless thing in the world; it likes to slither from one sacred bond to another, and it can't bear to settle in one place.

DON JUAN

And have I a right, do you think, to behave that way?

SGANARELLE

Well, Sir....

DON JUAN

What? Go on.

SGANARELLE

Certainly it's your right, if you insist; one wouldn't dare contradict you. But if you didn't insist, one might answer otherwise.

DON JUAN

Very well. I give you leave to speak freely, and to tell me what you truly feel.

a representation
of the current social state of mind

SGANARELLE

In that case, Sir, I'll tell you frankly that I don't approve your conduct in the least. I think it's shameful to love in all directions as you do.

DON JUAN

What! You'd have a man tie himself down to the first pretty woman who takes his fancy, and forsake the world for her, and never look at another? How absurd to make a specious virtue of fidelity, and bury oneself forever in a single passion, and be dead from youth onward to all the other beauties by whom one might be dazzled! No, no: constancy is for insensitive clods alone. All fair women have the right to enchant us, and the fact that we've met one of them first shouldn't deprive all the rest of their just claim on our hearts. For myself, I'm ravished by beauty wherever I find it, and I yield at once to the sweet violence with which it takes us captive. It's useless for me to pledge my heart and hand; the love I feel for one charming creature can't pledge me to be unjust to the others; I still have eyes for the merits of them all, and I render to each one the tribute that Nature exacts of us. I can't, in short, deny my heart to anything that strikes me as lovable, and the sight of a beautiful face so masters me that, if I had a thousand hearts, I'd give them all.

There is, besides, an inexpressible charm in the first stirrings of a new passion, and the whole pleasure of love lies in change. It's a delicious thing to subdue the heart of some young beauty by a hundred sweet attentions; to see yourself making some small progress with her every day; to combat her modest innocence, and her reluctance to surrender, with tears and sighs and rapturous speeches; to break through all her little defenses, one by one; to vanquish her cherished scruples, and gently bring her round to granting your desires. But once one is the master, there's nothing more to say or wish for: the joy of passionate pursuit is over, and all that remains is the boredom of a placid affection—until some new beauty appears and revives one's desires, enchanting the heart with the prospect of a new conquest. To be brief, then, there's nothing sweeter than overcoming the resistance of an attractive woman, and I bring to that enterprise the ambition of a conquering general, who moves on forever from victory to victory, and will set no limit to his longings. Nothing can withstand the impetuousness of my desires: I feel my heart capable of loving all the earth; and, like Alexander, I wish that there were still more worlds in which to wage my amorous campaigns.

SGANARELLE

Bless my soul, what a recitation! You seem to have learned all that by heart, and you talk just like a book.

DON JUAN

Well—what have you to say to it?

15

SGANARELLE

Heavens! I've a great deal to say, but I don't know how to
say it. You've twisted things in such a way as to make it
seem that you're in the right; and yet the fact is that
you're not. I was ready with the best arguments in the
world, and you've made a muddle of them. Well, let it go;
the next time I discuss anything with you, I'll put my
thoughts in writing before-hand.

DON JUAN

An excellent idea.

SGANARELLE

But Sir, if I still have your leave to speak out, may I say
that I'm more than a little scandalized by the life you
lead?

DON JUAN

What do you mean? What life do I lead?

SGANARELLE

A very good one. But, for example, your habit of marry-
ing a different person every month or so. . . .

DON JUAN

Could anything be more pleasant?

SGANARELLE

Yes, I can see that it's very pleasant and very amusing, and I could adjust to it, if there were no harm in it; but, Sir, to trifle so with a holy sacrament....

DON JUAN

Enough, enough. That's a matter between myself and Heaven, and Heaven and I will settle it very nicely without your fretting about it.

SGANARELLE

But, Sir, for mercy's sake! I've always heard that it's dangerous to make light of Heaven, and that freethinkers never come to a good end.

DON JUAN

Hold on there, Master Blockhead! Remember what I've told you. I don't like people who preach at me.

SGANARELLE

Oh, I wasn't speaking of you—God forbid! You, Sir, are a man who knows what he's doing, and if you don't believe in anything, you have your reasons. But there are, in this world, some rash little men who are freethinkers without knowing why, and who play at being unbelievers because they think it gives them style. If I had a master like that, I'd say to him flatly, looking him straight in the face, "How dare you scoff at Heaven as you do? How, without trembling, can you make mock of the most sacred things?

What right have you—little earthworm, little pigmy that
you are (I'm speaking to the master I mentioned), what
right have you to make a joke of what all men hold in rev-
erence? Do you think that because you have a title, and a
curly blonde wig, and feathers in your hat, and a gold-
embroidered coat, and flaming-red ribbons (I'm speaking
to that other person, not to you), do you think, I say, that
such things make you a great intellect, and that you're free
to act with absolute license, and that no one will dare confront you with the truth? Learn then from me, your valet,
that, sooner or later, Heaven will punish the impious man,
that an evil life leads to an evil death, and that...."

DON JUAN

Quiet!

SGANARELLE

What's the matter?

DON JUAN

What matters at present, I'll have you know, is that a
young beauty has stolen my heart, and that, drawn by her
many perfections, I've followed her to this town.

SGANARELLE

Have you no fears about returning here? It was here, Sir,
that you killed that Commander, six months ago.

DON JUAN

Why should I be afraid? Didn't I kill him properly?

SGANARELLE

Oh, very properly; a thorough job; he'd be wrong to complain.

DON JUAN

I've been given a full pardon for that affair.

SGANARELLE

Yes, but that pardon may not satisfy the vengeful feelings of his family and friends, and....

DON JUAN

Come, now, let's give no thought to the bad things that might happen to us; let's think only of what might bring us pleasure. The young beauty I mentioned, an utterly delectable creature, is engaged to be married, and she's been brought here to this town by her fiancé. Quite by chance I caught sight of these lovers elsewhere, three or four days before their coming here. Never had I seen two people so enchanted by each other, so radiantly in love. Their open tenderness and mutual delight moved me deeply; it pierced me to the heart, and aroused in me a love that was rooted in jealousy. Yes, from the moment I saw them I found their shared happiness intolerable; envy sharpened my desires, and with keenest pleasure I began to consider how I would mar their felicity, and disrupt a union which it pained my heart to behold. But thus far all my efforts have been in vain, and so I must resort to extreme measures. Today, our husband-to-be plans to entertain his lady with a pleasant sail upon the sea. Without telling you, I've made full preparations for achieving my desire; I've engaged a vessel, and hired a crew of men, and with these it should be quite simple for me to abduct my young beauty.

SGANARELLE

But, Sir!...

DON JUAN

Eh?

SGANARELLE

That's a capital idea; just what should be done. Nothing matters in this life but getting what one wants.

DON JUAN

Then get ready to accompany me, and make sure that you bring along all of my weapons, so that....
(*He sees Doña Elvira approaching.*)
Oh, what a tiresome interruption! Scoundrel, you didn't tell me that she also was in town.

SGANARELLE

You didn't ask me, Sir.

DON JUAN

Is she demented, not to have changed her dress, and to come to this place in her country clothes?

SCENE THREE

DOÑA ELVIRA, DON JUAN, SGANARELLE

DOÑA ELVIRA

Will you be so kind, Don Juan, as to acknowledge my presence? Will you not deign, at least, to turn your face this way?

DON JUAN

I must say, Madam, that you take me by surprise, and that I hadn't expected to see you here.

DOÑA ELVIRA

Yes, I see very clearly that you weren't expecting me; and you look surprised, indeed, but not in the way I'd hoped for. Your cold reaction, just now, gave me full proof of all that I've been refusing to believe. I wonder at my simple, foolish heart, which despite so much obvious evidence has persisted in doubting your treachery. I confess that I've been so silly, or rather so stupid, as to try to keep myself in the dark—to deny what my eyes and my judgement were telling me. I sought to explain away what it pained me to perceive, the lessening of your love for me; and I invented a hundred excuses for your abrupt departure, seeking to acquit you of the very crime with which my reason charged you. Day after day, I refused to listen to my own just suspicions, since to hear them would have made you guilty in my eyes. My heart harkened instead to a thousand foolish fantasies, all depicting you as innocent. But after this reception I can doubt no longer. The look with which I was greeted tells me more than I ever wished to know. Nevertheless, it would please me to hear from your own lips the reasons for your departure. Do speak, Don Juan, and let's see with what countenance you can justify your behavior.

DON JUAN

Sganarelle, Madam, will tell you my reasons for leaving.

SGANARELLE *(Aside to Don Juan.)*

I, Sir? If you please, Sir, I know nothing about them.

DOÑA ELVIRA

Very well, then: speak, Sganarelle. It doesn't matter from whose lips I hear those reasons.

DON JUAN *(Signaling Sganarelle to approach Doña Elvira.)*

Go on, now. Speak to Madam.

SGANARELLE *(Aside, to Don Juan.)*

What would you have me say?

DOÑA ELVIRA

Come here, since you're to be his spokesman, and give me some explanation of that hasty departure.

[*Act One • Scene Three*]

DON JUAN

Aren't you going to answer her?

SGANARELLE

I don't have any answers. You're just making a fool of
your poor servant.

DON JUAN

Answer the lady, I tell you.

SGANARELLE

Madam....

DOÑA ELVIRA

Yes?

SGANARELLE *(Turning toward his master.)*

Sir....

DON JUAN *(With a threatening gesture.)*

If you don't....

SGANARELLE

Madam, it was because of conquerors, and Alexander, and
the need of more worlds, that we had to leave. There, Sir;
that's all I could think of to say.

DOÑA ELVIRA

Will you be so kind, Don Juan, as to interpret those mysterious phrases?

DON JUAN

Madam, to tell the truth....

DOÑA ELVIRA

Oh, really! For a courtier, who ought to be used to this sort of thing, you're very bad at defending yourself. It's pitiable to see you so tongue-tied and abashed. Why don't you clothe your brow with a noble effrontery? Why don't you swear that your feelings for me are unchanged, that you love me still with a matchless passion, and that nothing but death could separate you from me? Why don't you tell me that affairs of the most urgent nature forced you to leave without bidding me farewell; that, much against your will, you're obliged to remain here for a time, and that I may return whence I came in the assurance that you'll follow me as soon as possible; that you truly burn to be with me again, and that when you're far from me, you suffer the anguish of a body that's been divided from its soul? That's the sort of thing you should say in your defense, rather than standing there speechless.

DON JUAN

I assure you, Madam, that I have no talent for dissembling, and that my heart is utterly sincere. I shan't tell you that my feelings are unchanged, and that I burn to be with you again, for the plain truth is that, when I took my departure, I was in flight from you—not at all for the reasons which you may imagine, but for pure reasons of conscience, and from a conviction that it would be sinful to live with you any longer. I'd begun to feel qualms about my conduct, Madam; I opened the eyes of my soul, and bade them look upon my actions. I faced the fact that, in order to make you my bride, I had stolen you from the holy seclusion of a convent, that you had broken the vows which pledged you to a purer life, and that Heaven is much incensed by such behavior. Remorse swept over me, and I feared the wrath of the Almighty. I now saw how our marriage was nothing but an adultery in disguise, that it would bring down some dire punishment on our heads, and that I must therefore try to forget you, and let you return to your first commitment. Surely, Madam, you won't find fault with so pious a decision, or wish me to incur the displeasure of Heaven by living with you now....

DOÑA ELVIRA

Ah, you scoundrel! I know you now, through and through—though, unhappily, that knowledge comes too late, and can serve only to fill me with despair. Be assured, however, that your crime won't go unpunished, and that the Heaven which you take so lightly will avenge me for your faithlessness.

DON JUAN

Heaven, Sganarelle!

SGANARELLE

Yes, we make fun of such things, you and I.

[*Act One • Scene Three*]

DON JUAN

Madam....

DOÑA ELVIRA

Enough. I'll hear no more of your speeches, and I blame myself for having listened so long. When one has been wronged and humiliated, it's base to discuss the matter; in such cases, a noble heart should act at once, without a lot of talk. Don't expect me to shower you now with revilements and reproaches: no, no, my wrath won't spend itself in empty words, and I'll reserve its full fury for the taking of my revenge. I tell you once again, faithless man, that Heaven will punish you for the wrong you've done me; and if you have no fear of Heaven, fear at least the anger of an outraged woman.

(She exits.)

SGANARELLE *(Aside.)*

If only he were capable of remorse!

DON JUAN *(After a moment's reflection.)*

Now then, let's go ahead with our amorous enterprise

SGANARELLE *(Alone.)*

Oh, what a wicked master I'm forced to serve!

ACT TWO

SCENE ONE

The countryside, near the seashore and not far from the city.

CHARLOTTE

Good gracious, Pierrot! I guess you got there in the nick
of time.

PIERROT

By golly, t'was only by a hair's breadth that them two
wasn't drownded.

CHARLOTTE

So, t'was that big wind this morning that turned 'em over
in the sea?

PIERROT

Listen, Charlotte, I can tell you the whole thing just like
it happened, for I was on the spot, like the fellow says,
and I was the one that spotted 'em first. There we was on
the seashore, me and fat Lucas, and we was fooling
around with some clods of dirt, chucking 'em at each
other's heads; I don't have to tell you how fat Lucas likes
to fool around, and sometimes I fool around myself. Well,
while we was fooling around, and chucking clods like I

29

said, I seen something far away that was wallowing in the water, and that kept coming towards us in lunges, you might say. I kept my eye right on it, and then suddenly I seen that I couldn't see it no more. "Hey, Lucas," I says, "I think some folks is swimming out there." "Come on," he says to me, "you've et some catnip and you're seeing things." "By gum," I told him, "there's nothing wrong with my eyes; there's men out there." "No sir," he says to me, "you've got the day-blindness." "Do you want to bet," I says, "that I ain't got no day-blindness," I says, "and that there's two men," I says, "swimming right this way?" "By jiminy," he says, "I'll bet you there ain't." "Well," says I, "I got ten sous that says there is." "I'll take that bet," he says, "and to show that I mean it," he says, "here's my money." Well, I was no fool, and no piker neither; I tossed down five sous, by golly, and five more sous in change, just as bold as I'd have tossed off a glass of wine—for I'm a taker of chances, and nothing holds me back. Anyway, I knew what I was doing. What a fool he was to take my bet! We'd hardly put our money down when two men was floating there in plain sight, waving their arms for us to come and get 'em; and so I bent down, first, and scooped up the stakes. "Come on, Lucas," I says to him, "you can see that they're hollering at us; let's go quick and rescue 'em." "No," says he, "they cost me money." Well, to make a long story short, I badgered him until we got ourselves into a rowboat, and then we hauled and heaved out to where we could pull 'em out of the water, and then we took 'em home to warm up by the fire, and they stripped stark naked so as to dry out, and then in come two more of the same crew, which had rescued themselves, and then Mathurine showed up, and one of 'em took to making eyes at her. There you are, Charlotte; that's how it all come to pass.

CHARLOTTE

Didn't you tell me, Pierrot, that one of 'em was a lot better looking than the others?

PIERROT

Yes, that one's the master. I figure he must be a big, big gentleman, because his clothes is all over gold from head to foot; and them that serve him is gentlemen too. Still and all, however big a gentleman he is, he'd 'a been drownded, by George, if I hadn't 'a been there.

CHARLOTTE

Just think of it!

PIERROT

Yes siree, if it hadn't 'a been for us, he'd 'a drunk his fill of the sea.

CHARLOTTE

Is he still in your house stark naked, Pierrot?

PIERROT

Nope. They put his clothes on again, right in front of us. Holy Smoke, I'd never seen one of that sort getting dressed before! What a lot of crazy doodads and contraptions these court gentlemen do put on! I'd get lost in all that stuff, myself, and it made me dizzy to look at it. Lord, Charlotte, they've got hair that comes on and off, and when they get dressed they put it on, last thing, like a

big straw nightcap. They've got shirts with sleeves so
wide that you and me together could crawl right into 'em.
Instead of breeches, they've got an apron big as from here
to Easter. Instead of a waistcoat, there's a little vest that
don't hardly come down to their belly. And instead of a
neckband there's a huge lace neckerchief, with four big
linen tassels hanging down in front. On top of that,
they've got frilly bands around their wrists, and big fun-
nels of lace on their legs, and everywhere there's so many
ribbons—so terrible many ribbons—that it's a disgrace.
There's even ribbons stuck all over their shoes, which if I
tried to wear 'em I'd fall down and break my neck.

CHARLOTTE

My goodness, Pierrot, I must go and have a look at some
of that.

PIERROT

No, wait a bit, Charlotte, and listen to me; I got something else to say to you, I do.

CHARLOTTE

Well, tell me. What is it?

PIERROT

Look here, Charlotte: like the fellow says, I got to get a
load off my mind. I love you; you know that; and I want
for us to get married. But, doggone it, I ain't satisfied
with you.

CHARLOTTE

You ain't? What's the trouble?

PIERROT

The trouble is that you grieve my heart, and that's the truth.

CHARLOTTE

How come? Why do I grieve you?

PIERROT

Because, dad blast it, you don't love me.

CHARLOTTE

Oh! Is that all?

PIERROT

Yes, that's all, and it's plenty.

CHARLOTTE

Land sakes, Pierrot, you're always telling me the same old story.

PIERROT

I always tell you the same old story because it always *is* the same old story; if it *wasn't* always the same old story, I wouldn't always be telling you the same old story.

CHARLOTTE

But what am I supposed to do? What do you want?

PIERROT

Damn it to hell, I want you to love me.

CHARLOTTE

And don't I love you?

PIERROT

No, you don't love me; and in spite of that, I do everything to make you care for me. I buy you ribbons—I ain't
complaining, now—I buy you ribbons from every peddler
that passes through; I break my neck robbing blackbirds'
nests for you; I have the fiddlers play for you when it's
your birthday. But in all that, it's as if I was banging my
head agin a wall. Doggone it, when a person loves you it
ain't fair or decent not to love him back.

CHARLOTTE

Oh, sakes alive, I *do* love you back.

PIERROT

Yes, yes, you love me in a mighty strange way.

CHARLOTTE

What do you want me to do?

PIERROT

I want you to act the way folks act when they love like they ought to.

CHARLOTTE

I don't love you like I ought to?

PIERROT

No. If you did, t'would be plain to see. When folks love a person truly, they play all kinds of monkey tricks on 'em. Think of that fat girl Thomasse, and how crazy she is for young Robin. She's always hanging 'round and pestering him, and she don't give him a moment's peace. She's always pulling some prank, or giving him a thump as she goes by. The other day, when he was setting on a stool, she yanked it out from under him, so that he fell down flat on his back. By jiminy, that's how it is when folks are in love. But you, you never say a word to me, you just stand there like a fence-post, and I could walk past you twenty times without you giving me the least little thump, or saying the least little thing. By gum, that just ain't human; you're too cold to a person.

CHARLOTTE

What d'you expect me to do? It's my nature, and I can't make myself over.

PIERROT

Your nature ain't no excuse. When humans feel affection for somebody, they always let it show a little.

CHARLOTTE

Well, I love you as much as I can, and if that don't satisfy you, you'd better go and love somebody else.

PIERROT

So, I've got my walking papers, eh? Damnation! If you loved me, could you say such a thing as that?

CHARLOTTE

Why did you pester me so, and get me all upset?

PIERROT

Hell's bells, what harm have I done you? All I ask from you is a little affection.

CHARLOTTE

Well, leave me alone, and don't press me too hard. Maybe t'will come over me all of a sudden, out of the blue.

PIERROT

Let's shake hands and make up, Charlotte.

CHARLOTTE

All right. There.

PIERROT

Promise that you'll try to love me a little more.

CHARLOTTE

I'll do my best, but it'll have to come of itself. Pierrot, is that the gentleman you was telling about?

PIERROT

Yep, that's him.

CHARLOTTE

Heavenly days, how fine-looking he is, and what a shame if he'd been drownded!

PIERROT

I'll be back in a few minutes; after all that hard rowing, I need a glass or two to get my strength back.

SCENE TWO

DON JUAN, SGANARELLE, CHARLOTTE
Charlotte only is at stage rear.

DON JUAN

Well, Sganarelle, we're failures. That sudden squall upset
both our boat and the clever plans we'd made. But to tell
you the truth, the peasant girl whom I left just now makes
up for our misfortune, and her charms have swept away
my chagrin at the sorry outcome of our adventure. I'm
resolved that her heart won't escape me; and I've already
worked upon her feelings, so that she won't resist my
sighs for long.

SGANARELLE

Sir, I confess that you astound me. An hour ago, we
barely escaped from death, yet instead of thanking
Heaven for the mercy it's shown us, you invite its wrath
by resuming your wilful ways and your amorous wick....
   (Don Juan gives him a threatening look.)
Hush, you officious knave! You don't know what you're
talking about, and your master knows what he's doing.
Mind your tongue.

[*Act Two • Scene Two*]

DON JUAN *(Seeing Charlotte.)*

Well, now! Whence comes this other country maid,
Sganarelle? Have you ever seen anything prettier? What
do you think—is this one the equal of the other?

SGANARELLE

Most certainly.
(Aside.)
One more victim.

DON JUAN *(To Charlotte.)*

What have I done, fair lady, to deserve this delightful encounter? Can it be that, in this rustic place, among these
rocks and trees, there are creatures who look like you?

CHARLOTTE

There are, Sir, like you see.

DON JUAN

Were you born in this village?

CHARLOTTE

Yes, Sir.

DON JUAN

And do you live here?

CHARLOTTE

Yes, Sir.

DON JUAN

And your name is....

CHARLOTTE

Charlotte. Your servant, Sir.

DON JUAN

Oh, what a beauty! And what flashing eyes she has!

CHARLOTTE

Sir, you're making me all embarrassed.

DON JUAN

Oh, you mustn't be embarrassed to hear the truth about yourself. What do you say, Sganarelle? Could anything be lovelier to look at? Turn around a little, if you will. Ah, what a dainty figure! Now lift your chin a little, please. Ah, what a sweet face! Open your eyes wide. Ah, how beautiful they are! Now let me have a look at your teeth, if you please. Ah, how fetching they are—and those lips, how desirable! For my part, I'm ravished; I've never seen anyone so charming.

CHARLOTTE

You're pleased to say so, Sir, but I wonder if you ain't just making fun of me.

DON JUAN

I make fun of you? God forbid! I love you too much for that, and whatever I say to you comes from the bottom of my heart.

CHARLOTTE

In that case, I'm much obliged.

DON JUAN

Not at all; you owe me nothing for the things I've said about you. It's only your beauty that you have to thank.

CHARLOTTE

Sir, your talk's too fancy for me, and I ain't got the wit to answer you back.

DON JUAN

Just look at her hands, Sganarelle.

CHARLOTTE

Oh, heavens, Sir! They're as black as I don't know what.

DON JUAN

Ha! What are you saying? They're the most beautiful hands in the world. Allow me to kiss them, I beg of you.

CHARLOTTE

You pay me a great honor, Sir, and if I'd known about this aforehand, I'd have given 'em a good scrubbing with bran.

DON JUAN

Now, tell me something, my pretty Charlotte: you're not married, I assume?

CHARLOTTE

No, Sir, but I soon will be—to Pierrot, who's the son of our neighbor, Simonette.

DON JUAN

What? Shall a person like you be the wife of a simple peasant? No, no: that would be a profanation of your beauty, and you weren't born to live in some country town. You deserve a better fate than that, and Heaven, which knows your worth, has expressly sent me here to prevent such a marriage, and do justice to your charms. In short, fair Charlotte, I love you with all my heart, and if you'll but say the word I shall snatch you away from this miserable place and raise you to the station where you belong. Doubtless my love seems rather sudden, but why should it not be? So great is your beauty, Charlotte, that you inspire as much love in ten minutes as another could do in half a year.

CHARLOTTE

Honest to goodness, Sir, I don't know what to do when
you carry on like that. The things you say are very nice,
and I'd give anything if I could believe them; but I've always been told that great gentlemen ain't to be trusted,
and that fine talkers like you are deceivers who only want
to seduce us girls and ruin us.

DON JUAN

I'm not that sort of man.

SGANARELLE *(Aside.)*

Oh, no! Perish the thought!

CHARLOTTE

Look here, Sir, it's no joke when a girl lets herself be ruined. I'm a poor country girl, but my honor is precious to
me, and I'd sooner be dead than see myself disgraced.

DON JUAN

Could I be so wicked as to deceive a young woman like
you? Could I be so base as to besmirch your honor? No,
no: I've too much conscience for that. I love you, Charlotte, and my intentions are wholly honorable; to show
you that I mean what I say, let me inform you that the one
thing I desire is to marry you. What greater proof could
there be of my sincerity? I stand ready to wed you, whenever you wish; and let this man here be witness to the
promise I make you.

SGANARELLE

Oh, yes, never fear: he'll marry you as much as you like.

DON JUAN

Ah, Charlotte, I can see that you still don't understand
me. You do me a great wrong when you judge me by
other men; if there are knaves among mankind whose
only thought is to seduce young women, you must not
think of me as one of them, or doubt the sincerity of my
word. In any case, you should feel secure in your beauty.
When one has a face like yours, one should be above all
common fears. You bear no resemblance, I assure you, to
the sort of girl whom men deceive and cast aside; and I
swear that, if the thought of betraying you crossed my
mind, I'd pierce myself to the heart a thousand times.

CHARLOTTE

Heavens alive! I don't know whether you're telling the
truth or not, but you make a body believe you.

DON JUAN

Now that you believe me, and give me the trust I deserve,
let me repeat the promise that I made you. Won't you accept my offer, and consent to be my wife?

CHARLOTTE

Yes, so long as my aunt says I can.

DON JUAN

Your hand on it then, Charlotte, since for your part you
see no obstacle.

CHARLOTTE

But please, Sir, don't go and deceive me; that would give
you a bad conscience, for you see how I'm trusting you.

DON JUAN

What's this? It seems that you still doubt my sincerity!
Would you have me swear some terrible oath or other?
May Heaven....

CHARLOTTE

Oh, mercy! Don't swear, I'll believe you.

DON JUAN

Then give me a little kiss to seal our engagement.

CHARLOTTE

Oh, Sir! I beg you, wait until we're married and all; after
that, I'll kiss you as much as you want.

DON JUAN

Very well, fair Charlotte, your wish shall be my law. But
do at least yield me your hand, and let me express my rap-
ture by a thousand kisses....

SCENE THREE

DON JUAN, SGANARELLE, PIERROT, CHARLOTTE

PIERROT *(Stepping between the two,
and pushing Don Juan backwards.)*

Hold on there, Sir; go easy, if you please. You're getting
overheated, and you might catch your death of something.

DON JUAN *(Giving Pierrot a hard shove.)*

Why does this low-brow interfere?

PIERROT *(Jumping back between Don Juan and Charlotte.)*

Keep your hands off, I tell you, and don't be kissing our
fiancées.

DON JUAN *(Pushing him again.)*

Oh, how noisy he is!

PIERROT

Hang it! You hadn't ought to push people like that.

CHARLOTTE *(Catching Pierrot by the arm.)*

Leave him alone, now, Pierrot.

PIERROT

What? Leave him alone? I ain't a-going to.

DON JUAN

No?

PIERROT

By gar! Just because you're a fine gentleman, you think you can come here and kiss our women right under our noses. Go kiss your own women.

DON JUAN

You mean that?

PIERROT

I mean that.
                    (*Don Juan slaps him in the face.*)
Damnation, don't hit me!
                    (*Another slap.*)
Ouch, doggone it!
                    (*Another slap.*)
Goldarn it!
                    (*Another slap.*)
Drat and thunderation! It ain't right to beat people, and it's a fine reward to give a person who saved you from being drownded.

CHARLOTTE

Now, Pierrot, don't get sore.

47

PIERROT

I sure as heck *will* get sore; and you're a slut, you are, to let yourself get trifled with.

CHARLOTTE

Oh, Pierrot, it ain't like you think it is. This gentleman wants to marry me, and so you've got nothing to be upset about.

PIERROT

What do you mean? Damn it, you're engaged to me.

CHARLOTTE

That don't matter, Pierrot. If you love me, shouldn't it make you happy that I'm going to be a lady?

PIERROT

By golly, no! I'd sooner see you dead than belonging to somebody else.

CHARLOTTE

Now, now, Pierrot, don't get all worked up: if I get to be a lady, there'll be something in it for you. You can supply our house with butter and cheese.

PIERROT

By gar, I won't supply you with nothing ever, not even if you pay me double. So this is what comes of you listening

to that feller's talk! Damme, if I'd known that a while ago,
I wouldn't have pulled him out of the water; I'd have
knocked him over the head with an oar.

DON JUAN (*Approaching Pierrot,
with a hand raised to strike him.*)

What did you say?

PIERROT (*Backing off, slipping behind Charlotte.*)

By gar, I ain't afeared of nobody.

DON JUAN (*Moving around Charlotte, pursuing Pierrot.*)

Just wait till I catch you.

PIERROT (*Moving around to Charlotte's other side.*)

I ain't scared of nothing, not me.

DON JUAN (*Following after Pierrot.*)

We shall see.

PIERROT (*Once more taking refuge behind Charlotte.*)

I've stood up to many of your sort.

DON JUAN

Hah!

[Act Two • Scene Three]

SGANARELLE

Oh, Sir, leave the poor wretch alone. T'would be a sin to beat him.
(To Pierrot, stepping between him and Don Juan.)
Listen, my poor boy: be off with you, and say no more to him.

PIERROT *(Stepping around Sganarelle and boldly addressing Don Juan.)*

I've got more to say to him, and I'm going to say it!

DON JUAN *(Raising his hand to slap Pierrot, who ducks his head so that Sganarelle receives the blow.)*

Ha! I'll teach you.

SGANARELLE *(Looking at Pierrot, who has bent over to avoid the slap.)*

A curse on that yokel!

DON JUAN *(To Sganarelle.)*

There's the reward for your charity.

PIERROT

By jeepers, I'm going to tell her aunt about all this funny-business.
(He exits.)

DON JUAN (*To Charlotte.*)

Now then, Charlotte: I'm soon to be the most fortunate of men, and I wouldn't exchange my happiness for anything in creation. How delicious our married life is going to be, and how....

SCENE FOUR

DON JUAN, SGANARELLE, CHARLOTTE, MATHURINE

SGANARELLE *(Who sees Mathurine approaching.)*

Oh, no!

MATHURINE *(To Don Juan.)*

Why, Sir! What are you doing here with Charlotte? Are you making love to her too?

DON JUAN *(Aside to Mathurine.)*

No, quite the reverse. She expressed, just now, a wish to be my wife, and I was informing her of my engagement to you.

CHARLOTTE *(To Don Juan.)*

What does that Mathurine want of you?

DON JUAN *(Aside to Charlotte.)*

She's jealous because she found me talking to you, and she wants me to marry her; but I've told her that it's you I care for.

[*Act Two • Scene Four*]

MATHURINE

Look here, Charlotte....

DON JUAN (*Aside to Mathurine.*)

Anything you say to her will be a waste of time; she's obsessed with that wild notion.

CHARLOTTE

Listen, Mathurine....

DON JUAN (*Aside to Charlotte.*)

T'will be useless for you to talk with her; she won't give up that fantasy.

MATHURINE

If you don't mind....

DON JUAN (*Aside to Mathurine.*)

There's no way to make her listen to reason.

CHARLOTTE

I'd like to know....

DON JUAN (*Aside to Charlotte.*)

She's as stubborn as the Devil himself.

[*Act Two • Scene Four*]

MATHURINE

Do you honestly....

DON JUAN *(Aside to Mathurine.)*

Don't bother with her; she's mad.

CHARLOTTE

If you ask me....

DON JUAN *(Aside to Charlotte.)*

Let her be; she's quite demented.

MATHURINE

No, no, I've got to talk with her.

CHARLOTTE

I want to know what she thinks she's doing.

MATHURINE

Why?...

DON JUAN *(Aside to Mathurine.)*

She'll claim, I wager, that I've promised to marry her.

CHARLOTTE

I....

[*Act Two • Scene Four*]

DON JUAN (*Aside to Charlotte.*)

It's a safe bet that she'll tell you how I've sworn to make her my wife.

MATHURINE

Listen, Charlotte, it ain't fair for you to horn in on my affairs.

CHARLOTTE

You've got no right to get jealous, Mathurine, when this gentleman talks to me.

MATHURINE

The gentleman saw me first.

CHARLOTTE

If he saw you first, he saw me second, and he's promised to marry me.

DON JUAN (*Aside to Mathurine.*)

There! What did I tell you?

MATHURINE (*To Charlotte.*)

Go on with you. It's me, and not you, that he's promised to marry.

DON JUAN *(Aside to Charlotte.)*

Just as I predicted!

CHARLOTTE

Go tell that to the birds; it's me, like I said.

MATHURINE

You're joking. I tell you again, it's me.

CHARLOTTE

This gentleman can say if I'm right or not.

MATHURINE

This gentleman can correct me if I'm wrong.

CHARLOTTE

Sir, is it true that you promised to marry her?

DON JUAN *(Aside to Charlotte.)*

You can't be serious.

MATHURINE

Sir, did you give your word to be her husband?

[*Act Two • Scene Four*]

DON JUAN *(Aside to Mathurine.)*

How can you think such a thing?

CHARLOTTE

You see how she keeps insisting.

DON JUAN *(Aside to Charlotte.)*

Let her insist.

MATHURINE

She won't stop saying it.

DON JUAN *(Aside to Mathurine.)*

Let her talk.

CHARLOTTE

No, no, let's have the truth.

MATHURINE

It's got to be decided.

CHARLOTTE

Yes, Mathurine, I want this gentleman to show you up for a silly goose.

MATHURINE

Yes, Charlotte, I want this gentleman to take you down a peg.

CHARLOTTE

You'll see.

MATHURINE *(To Charlotte.)*

It's you that'll see.

CHARLOTTE *(To Don Juan.)*

Speak, Sir.

MATHURINE *(To Don Juan.)*

Tell us.

DON JUAN *(Flustered, and addressing them both at once.)*

What would you have me say? Both of you contend that I've promised to marry you. Since each of you knows what I really said, why need I explain myself further? Why force me to repeat myself? The one to whom, in fact, I gave my promise should be able to laugh off the pretensions of the other; nothing should trouble her, provided I keep my word. But all this talk accomplishes nothing; it's actions that count, not words, and it's by deeds, not speeches, that matters are decided. It's in that concrete sense that I shall settle this affair, and it will be clear, when I marry, which of you two has won my heart.

(Aside to Mathurine.)

Let her believe what she likes.

(Aside to Charlotte.)

Let her enjoy her fantasies.

(Aside to Mathurine.)

I adore you.

(Aside to Charlotte.)

I am your slave.

(Aside to Mathurine.)

All faces are ugly, compared to yours.

(Aside to Charlotte.)

Once one has seen you, one can't bear the sight of others.
I have one or two little orders to give; I shall be back with
you in a quarter-hour.

(He exits.)

CHARLOTTE *(To Mathurine.)*

Well, anyway I'm the one he loves.

MATHURINE *(To Charlotte.)*

It's me he's going to marry.

SGANARELLE

Ah, you poor girls, I pity your innocence, and I can't bear
to see you in such a hurry to be undone. Take my advice,
both of you: don't let yourselves be led astray by all the
lies you've been hearing: stay here in your little village,
and be safe.

[Act Two • Scene Four]

DON JUAN *(Speaking to himself, as he reenters.)*

Why didn't Sganarelle follow me, I wonder? What can he be doing?

SGANARELLE *(To the girls.)*

My master is a trickster. All he wants is to seduce you, as he has so many others. He's quite ready to marry the whole human race: he....
(He notices Don Juan.)
All that, of course, is false, and if anyone says those things to you, you must tell him that he is a liar. My master is not prepared to marry the whole human race, he is not a trickster, he has no intention of deceiving you, and he has never seduced anybody. But ah, here he is! If you don't believe me, ask him.

DON JUAN *(Eyeing Sganarelle, and suspicious of what he may have said.)*

By all means.

SGANARELLE

Sir, since the world is full of slanders, I've been anticipating what malicious tongues might say; and I've told these young ladies that if anyone speaks ill of you, they must re fuse to believe him, and tell him flatly that he's a liar.

DON JUAN

Sganarelle!

[*Act Two • Scene Four*]

SGANARELLE *(To Charlotte and Mathurine.)*

Yes, my master is a man of honor, I can vouch for that.

DON JUAN

Ahem!

SGANARELLE

His detractors are wicked men.

SCENE FIVE

DON JUAN, LA RAMÉE, CHARLOTTE, MATHURINE, SGANARELLE

LA RAMÉE *(Aside to Don Juan.)*

Sir, I've come to warn you that you're not safe in these parts.

DON JUAN

How's that?

LA RAMÉE

Twelve men on horseback are hunting for you, and they could arrive here at any moment. I don't know how they've managed to trace you, but I got this news from a peasant they'd questioned and to whom they'd given your description. There's no time to lose, and the quicker you get out of here, the better.

DON JUAN *(To Charlotte and Mathurine.)*

A pressing matter obliges me to go, now; but remember the promise I gave you, and be assured that you'll hear from me before tomorrow evening.
(Exeunt Charlotte and Mathurine.)
Since we're so outnumbered by our foes, I shall have to resort to cunning, and escape this danger by means of

some stratagem. Let me see: I'll have Sganarelle put on my clothes, and....

SGANARELLE

Oh, Sir, you're only joking. If I were in your clothes, someone might kill me, and....

DON JUAN

Come now, be quick. I offer you a very great honor; it's a lucky valet who can have the glory of dying for his master.

SGANARELLE

For such an honor, I can't thank you enough.
(Alone.)
O Heaven, if there's dying to be done, don't let me die of mistaken identity.

ACT THREE

SCENE ONE

DON JUAN—in country clothing.
SGANARELLE—in the garb of a doctor.
A forest near the sea, and not far from the town.

SGANARELLE

You must admit that I was right, Sir, and that both of us
are now admirably disguised. Your first idea wasn't at all
practical, and these costumes are far better camouflage
than what you had in mind.

DON JUAN

You look quite marvelous, it's true; I can't imagine where
you dug up that ridiculous garment.

SGANARELLE

Really? It's the professional gown of an old doctor, which
I picked up at a pawnshop, and which cost me a good bit
of money. Would you believe, Sir, that this gown has already brought me many signs of respect, that people bow
to me as I pass, and that they consult me as if I were a
learnèd man?

DON JUAN

They do? On what subjects?

SGANARELLE

Five or six peasants, both men and women, have run up to me when they saw me coming by, and asked my advice about one sickness or another.

DON JUAN

You told them, I suppose, that you knew nothing of medicine?

SGANARELLE

Why, certainly not. I felt I should uphold the honor of my gown, and so I pondered their symptoms and in each case prescribed some treatment.

DON JUAN

And what remedies did you prescribe?

SGANARELLE

Good Lord, Sir, I just said whatever came into my head; I tossed off prescriptions at random. It would be a funny thing, wouldn't it, if the sick actually got well, and came to thank me for healing them?

DON JUAN

Why shouldn't they? Why shouldn't you have the same rewards as all the other doctors? They do no more than you to heal the sick, and their science is purest humbug. The one thing they know how to do is to take credit when patients get better; and you should profit, as they do, from the gratitude of those who ascribe to your remedies what they really owe to Nature and good fortune.

SGANARELLE

What, Sir! Are you irreverent about medicine as well?

DON JUAN

It's one of the worst superstitions of mankind.

SGANARELLE

You don't believe, then, in senna, or cassia, or emetic wine?

DON JUAN

Why would you have me believe in such things?

SGANARELLE

You have a very doubting nature. But surely you know that, for some time, there's been great public excitement about emetic wine. Its miraculous effects have won over the most skeptical, and I myself, not three weeks ago, witnessed a wonderful proof of its virtue.

DON JUAN

How so?

SGANARELLE

There was a man who, for six whole days, had lain at death's door. All remedies had failed, and no one knew what else to do for him. At last, they decided to give him some emetic wine.

DON JUAN

And he recovered, did he?

SGANARELLE

No, he died.

DON JUAN

A wondrous result!

SGANARELLE

It certainly was! For six whole days he'd been unable to die, and it finished him off in a minute. What could be more effective?

DON JUAN

What, indeed?

SGANARELLE

But let's drop the subject of medicine, since you don't believe in it, and talk of other things. This costume has sharpened my wits, and I feel in the mood to debate.

You'll recall that you allow me to debate with you, and that the only thing you forbid is preaching.

DON JUAN

Very well, go ahead.

SGANARELLE

I just want to know your thoughts about some fundamental questions. Is it possible that you don't believe in Heaven at all?

DON JUAN

Let's table that question.

SGANARELLE

In other words, you don't. What about Hell?

DON JUAN

Huh!

SGANARELLE

Same answer. And the Devil, do you believe in him?

DON JUAN

Yes, yes.

SGANARELLE

So you doubt him too. Have you no faith whatever in the
life to come?

DON JUAN

Come, come.

SGANARELLE *(Aside.)*

I can see that I'm going to have trouble converting this
man.
(To Don Juan.)
Tell me, now: what are your beliefs regarding the Bogeyman? What about him, eh?

DON JUAN

Don't be an idiot.

SGANARELLE

Now, there you go too far, for there's nothing truer in
this world than the Bogeyman; I'll stake my life on that.
But one has to believe in something; what is it that you
believe?

DON JUAN

What do I believe?

SGANARELLE

Yes.

DON JUAN

I believe that two and two are four, Sganarelle, and that four and four are eight.

SGANARELLE

What a fine creed that is! So far as I can see, your religion consists of arithmetic. Men, I must say, can get some weird notions in their heads, and people who've studied a lot aren't always a lot wiser. As for me, Sir, I've never studied like you, thank God, and no one can boast of having taught me anything; but with my small wits, and my small judgement, I see things more clearly than all those books do, and I know for certain that this world we behold is not a mushroom that shot up overnight of its own doing. I'd like to ask you who made those trees, those rocks, this earth, and the sky we see up there, and if all those things created themselves? Look at yourself, for example; here you are: did you make yourself singlehanded, or wasn't it necessary for your father to beget you on your mother before you could exist? Can you look at all the inventions which compose the human apparatus, without marveling at the way they're designed to work together, one with the other? These nerves, these bones, these veins, these arteries, these... this lung, this heart, this liver, and all the other ingredients which are in there, and which.... Oh, my God, interrupt me, won't you? I can't argue if I'm not interrupted. You're deliberately keeping quiet, and you're letting me run on out of sheer malice.

DON JUAN

I'm waiting for your argument to be finished.

SGANARELLE

My argument, whatever you may say, is that there's something wonderful in man which all the wise heads can't explain. Isn't it marvelous that I'm here, and that I have something in my head that can think a hundred different things in a second, and can make my body do whatever it likes? I can choose to clap my hands, lift my arms, raise my eyes to Heaven, bow my head, shift my feet, move to the right, to the left, forward, backward, turn around....
(In turning around, he falls down.)

DON JUAN

Good! There lies your argument with a broken nose.

SGANARELLE

Curses! I'm a fool to waste my time arguing with you. Believe what you like: a lot I care if you're damned!

DON JUAN

What with all this reasoning, I think we've lost our way. Give a shout to that man over there, and ask him for directions.

SGANARELLE

Ho there, my man! Ho there, fellow! Ho, my friend! A word with you, if you please.

SCENE TWO

SGANARELLE

Kindly tell us by what route we may get to the town.

THE POOR MAN

You've only to follow this road, Sirs, and bear to the right when you come out of the woods. I warn you, however, to be on your guard, because for some time there have been robbers hereabouts.

DON JUAN

I'm much obliged to you, my friend, and I thank you with all my heart.

THE POOR MAN

Would you be so good, Sir, as to spare me some alms?

DON JUAN

Aha! You charge for your advice, I see.

[*Act Three* • *Scene Two*]

THE POOR MAN

I'm a poor man, Sir, who for ten years has lived all alone in these woods. I shall ask Heaven, in my prayers, to give you every good thing.

DON JUAN

Huh! Ask Heaven to give you a warm coat, and don't trouble so about the needs of others.

SGANARELLE *(To the Poor Man.)*

You don't know this gentleman, my good fellow: he believes only in two-and-two-are-four, and in four-and-four-are-eight.

DON JUAN

What's your occupation, here among these trees?

THE POOR MAN

I pray to Heaven, all day long, for the prosperity of the good, charitable people who have helped me.

DON JUAN

I assume, then, that you live very comfortably?

THE POOR MAN

Alas, Sir! I live in the greatest possible privation.

DON JUAN

You can't be serious; a man who prays to Heaven all day is bound to be well taken care of.

THE POOR MAN

I assure you, Sir, that most of the time I haven't a crust of bread to chew on.

DON JUAN

It's strange that you should be so shabbily rewarded for all your trouble. See here, I'll give you a gold Louis right now, if you'll just utter one blasphemous oath.

THE POOR MAN

Take the Lord's name in vain? Sir, would you have me commit such a sin?

DON JUAN

It's up to you. Do you want to earn a gold piece or not? Here's one that I'll give you, if you'll just swear that oath. Come now, let's hear it.

THE POOR MAN

Sir. . . .

DON JUAN

You can't have this unless you do.

SGANARELLE

Go on, blaspheme a little. It'll do no harm.

DON JUAN

Here it is, take it, take it. Take it, I tell you. But first you
must blaspheme.

THE POOR MAN

No, Sir, I'd rather starve to death.

DON JUAN

Well then, I'll give it to you for the love of humanity. But
what do I see over there? One man set upon by three others? That's not a fair contest, and I mustn't permit such
dastardly behavior.

SCENE THREE

SGANARELLE *(Alone.)*

My master is a real madman, to go looking for danger when it's not looking for him. But, my word! His intervention has tipped the balance, and the two of them have put the three to flight.

DON CARLOS *(With sword in hand.)*

It's plain to see, from the way those robbers fled, what help your strong arm gave me. Allow me, Sir, to thank you for a most courageous action, which....

DON JUAN *(Returning, sword in hand.)*

I did nothing, Sir, that you wouldn't have done in my place. One's own honor is challenged when one sees another in such a plight, and not to oppose the base actions of those rogues would have made me their accomplice. But how did you happen to fall into their hands?

DON CARLOS

I had by chance become separated from my brother, and the rest of our party; and as I was seeking to rejoin them I encountered those brigands, who began by killing my horse and, but for your brave assistance, would have done the same to me.

DON JUAN

Is your party going in the direction of the town?

DON CARLOS

Yes, though we don't intend to enter it; my brother and I must keep to the countryside, because we're involved in one of those vexing affairs wherein a gentleman must sacrifice himself and his family to the tyranny of honor. In such matters, the most fortunate outcome is still a disaster, for if one doesn't lose one's life one must lose one's country, and be thrust into exile. It is, I think, an unfortunate thing to be a gentleman, who can't rest secure in the wisdom and prudence of his own conduct, but is bound by the laws of honor to punish the misconduct of others. Our lives, our fortunes, and our peace of mind are at the mercy of any fool who deals us one of those insults which oblige a man of honor to fight to the death.

DON JUAN

Well, there's this compensation—that those so foolish as to do us wrong must suffer the same danger and distress of mind as we. But would it be indiscreet to ask the nature of this affair you mention?

DON CARLOS

The matter can't be kept secret for much longer; and since the affront to our family will soon be public knowledge, honor lies not in concealing our shame but in openly declaring our intent to be avenged. Therefore, Sir, I don't hesitate to tell you that the wrong we mean to avenge is the seduction of our sister and her abduction from a convent, and the wrongdoer is one Don Juan Tenorio, the son of Don Luis Tenorio. We've been seeking him for several days now, and this morning we picked up his trail, informed by a lackey that he'd ridden out along this coast with a company of four or five men. But all our searching has been fruitless, and we've no idea what's become of him.

DON JUAN

This Don Juan of whom you speak—do you know him, Sir?

DON CARLOS

Not personally, no. I've never seen him, and I know him only through my brother's descriptions of him; but his reputation is by no means good, and he's a man whose life....

DON JUAN

If you please, Sir, say no more. He is something of a friend of mine, and it would be cowardly of me to stand by and hear him denigrated.

DON CARLOS

For your sake, Sir, I'll say not a word more about him. The least I can do for you, since you've saved my life, is to hold my peace in your presence about a man whom you know, and of whom I can't speak without speaking ill.

But, friend though he may be, I hope that you don't approve his actions, or think it strange that we should seek vengeance on their account.

DON JUAN

On the contrary, I want to be of service in your quest, and spare you some unnecessary trouble. I'm a friend of Don Juan, I can't help that; but he mustn't expect to offend good gentlemen with impunity, and I promise to make him give you satisfaction.

DON CARLOS

For such great wrongs, what satisfaction could be given?

DON JUAN

Whatever your family honor may require. What's more, to save you the bother of a further search for Don Juan, I take it upon myself to produce him at whatever place you wish, and at whatever time you choose.

DON CARLOS

That promise, Sir, is balm to our offended hearts; but in view of what I owe you, it would much distress me if you yourself took part in the encounter.

DON JUAN

I'm so attached to Don Juan that he could never fight without my fighting also. In any case, I can answer for him as for myself, and if you'll just name a time and place, he'll appear and satisfy your honor.

DON CARLOS

Oh, what a cruel twist of fate! Why must I owe my life to you, when Don Juan is one of your friends?

SCENE FOUR

DON ALONSO AND THREE ATTENDANTS,
DON CARLOS, DON JUAN, SGANARELLE

DON ALONSO *(Speaking to his attendants,
not seeing Don Carlos or Don Juan.)*

Water my horses over there, then bring them along behind; I want to go on foot awhile.
(Perceiving the two men.)
Great God, what do I see? You, Brother, conversing with
our mortal enemy!

DON CARLOS

Our mortal enemy?

DON JUAN *(Backing off several paces,
and proudly placing a hand on his sword-hilt.)*

Yes, I myself am Don Juan. Though you outnumber me,
I shan't deny my name.

DON ALONSO *(Drawing his sword.)*

Ah, treacherous villain, you must die! Prepare....
(Sganarelle runs away to hide.)

DON CARLOS

No, Brother, hold! I'm indebted to him for my life; without the help of his arm, I'd have been killed by some brigands who fell upon me.

DON ALONSO

And should that fact stand in the way of our revenge? Whatever services a foe may render, he can't thereby disarm our enmity. Compare your debt to him with his offenses, Brother, and any gratitude must seem absurd. Since honor's infinitely more precious than life, we owe nothing to a man who has saved your life but robbed us of our honor.

DON CARLOS

As between life and honor, Brother, I well know which a gentleman must value more, and my debt of gratitude in no way lessens my wrath at his misdeeds. But permit me now to return what he has lent me, and pay him back at once for the life I owe him: let me postpone our vengeance, and grant him a few days in which to enjoy the fruits of his good deed.

DON ALONSO

No, no, if we put off our vengeance we shall run the risk of losing it; there might never be another chance. Heaven offers us this opportunity, and we must seize it. When one's honor has been mortally wounded, one should not respond with timid half-measures; if you have no stomach for what must be done, then step aside, and leave our glorious retribution to my sword alone.

DON CARLOS

Brother, I beg you....

DON ALONSO

All this talk is pointless; the man must die.

DON CARLOS

Stop, Brother; stop, I tell you. I shan't allow his blood to be spilt, and I swear by Heaven to defend him against any man, shielding him with the very life he saved. If your sword would reach him, it must first run me through.

DON ALONSO

So, you take our enemy's side against me! And, far from sharing the rage I feel at the sight of him, you treat him with a sweet solicitude!

DON CARLOS

Brother, let's achieve our just end in a moderate spirit, and not avenge our honor with such fury as you now display. Let's be the masters of our courage, and let our valor have nothing savage in it; let's be moved to action by the calm use of our reason, and not by blind passion. I don't wish, Brother, to be obligated to my enemy, and so I ask that, first of all, I may discharge my debt to him. Our vengeance will lose no lustre by having been deferred: on the contrary, it will gain in glory, and our having passed up this chance will make it appear more just in the world's eyes.

DON ALONSO

Oh, what utter folly, what delusion, to endanger the cause of one's honor for the sake of a fancied obligation!

DON CARLOS

Don't worry, Brother. If I'm making a mistake, I shall know how to rectify it, and I take upon myself a full responsibility for our cause: I know what our honor asks of us, and this one-day's delay, which my gratitude requires, will only increase my determination to meet its demands. Don Juan, you see that I'm at pains to return the good deed you did me, and you should judge my character by that, and know that I discharge all my debts with the same zeal; believe me, I shall repay the injury as scrupulously as I've repaid the kindness. I've no wish to force you, here and now, to declare your intentions, and you are free to consider, at leisure, the decisions that you must make. You well know the magnitude of the offense that you've given, and you may judge for yourself what reparations are called for. There are peaceful means by which you might satisfy us, and there are others both violent and bloody. But whatever you may decide, I have your word that you'll make Don Juan give me satisfaction; remember to do so, I pray you, and remember also that, from this moment on, my only debt is to my honor.

[*Act Three • Scene Four*]

DON JUAN

I didn't plead for this delay, and I shall keep my promise.

DON CARLOS

Let's go, Brother; a moment's clemency won't impair our stern resolve to do our duty.

SCENE FIVE

DON JUAN, SGANARELLE

DON JUAN

Ho there! I say! Sganarelle!

SGANARELLE *(Coming out of hiding.)*

You called?

DON JUAN

So, you knave! When I'm attacked, you run away, do you?

SGANARELLE

Pardon me, Sir; I had to slip into the bushes. I think that this gown has medicinal virtues, and that to wear it is like taking a laxative.

DON JUAN

A plague on your impudence! Do at least cloak your cowardice in a better lie than that. Do you know who he was, the man whose life I saved just now?

SGANARELLE

Do I know him? No.

DON JUAN

He's one of Elvira's brothers.

SGANARELLE

One of her bro...!

DON JUAN

He's a decent man; he behaved rather well, and I'm sorry
to be at odds with him.

SGANARELLE

You could easily settle all this in a peaceful way.

DON JUAN

Yes, but my passion for Doña Elvira has expired, and it
doesn't suit me to be tied down. I like to be free in love,
as you know, and I could never confine my heart within
four walls. As I've told you many a time, it's my nature to
yield to whatever bewitches my eye. My heart belongs to
all beautiful women, and it's their business to claim it,
each in her turn, and to keep it as long as they can. But
what's the grand edifice that I see between those trees?

SGANARELLE

You don't know?

[*Act Three • Scene Five*]

DON JUAN

No, I don't.

SGANARELLE

Why, Sir! It's the tomb that the Commander was having built, at the time when you killed him.

DON JUAN

Ah, yes; quite so. I didn't know that it was in this location. Everyone's told me of its wondrous architecture, and of the Commander's statue; I'd like to have a look at it.

SGANARELLE

Oh, Sir, don't go in there.

DON JUAN

Why not?

SGANARELLE

It's not seemly to call on a man whom you've killed.

DON JUAN

On the contrary, my visit will do him a courtesy, and if he's a man of breeding, he'll receive me graciously. Come, let's go in.
(The tomb opens, revealing a splendid mausoleum and the Statue of the Commander.)

SGANARELLE

Oh, how beautiful it is! What beautiful statues! And the beautiful marble! The beautiful columns! Oh, how beautiful it is! What do you think of it, Sir?

DON JUAN

I think that a dead man's vanity could scarcely go farther than this. Strange that a man who, while he lived, was content with a modest dwelling, should desire such a mansion when he needs a house no longer.

SGANARELLE

Here's the statue of the Commander.

DON JUAN

Dear God! How ridiculous he looks, got up like a Roman emperor!

SGANARELLE

My word, Sir, what a fine likeness it is! It's as if he were alive, and about to speak. The way he's looking at us would scare me, if I were alone, and I think he's not pleased to see us.

DON JUAN

He'd be wrong to glower at us; t'would be a poor way to acknowledge the honor of my visit. Ask him if he'd care to come and have dinner with me.

[*Act Three • Scene Five*]

SGANARELLE

Dinner, I think, is something he no longer needs.

DON JUAN

Ask him, I tell you.

SGANARELLE

You're not serious. I'd be crazy if I went and talked to a statue.

DON JUAN

Do as I tell you.

SGANARELLE

What a curious whim! My lord Commander...
(Aside.)
I can't help laughing at what I'm doing, but my master's making me do it.
(Aloud.)
My lord Commander, my master Don Juan asks that you do him the honor of joining him for dinner.
(The Statue nods its head.)
Aagh!

DON JUAN

What is it? What's the matter? Speak up, will you?

[*Act Three* • *Scene Five*]

SGANARELLE *(Nodding his head as the Statue did.)*

The Statue....

DON JUAN

Come, knave, what are you trying to say?

SGANARELLE

The Statue, I tell you....

DON JUAN

Well, what about the Statue? Out with it, or I'll break your neck.

SGANARELLE

The Statue nodded its head.

DON JUAN

The Devil take this idiot.

SGANARELLE

It nodded at me, I tell you: that's the God's honest truth. Go on and speak to it yourself, if you doubt me. Maybe you'll....

DON JUAN

Come here, you wretch, come here. I'll make you ashamed of your craven fantasies. Now, watch. Will my lord Commander be so kind as to come and dine with me?

(*The Statue nods its head once more.*)

SGANARELLE

I wouldn't have missed that for ten pistoles. Well, Sir?

DON JUAN

Come, let's get out of here.

SGANARELLE *(Alone.)*

So much for your free-thinkers, who won't believe in anything!

ACT FOUR

SCENE ONE

DON JUAN, SGANARELLE, RAGOTIN
Don Juan's residence.

DON JUAN

Whatever may have happened, let's say no more about
that trivial incident. Most likely we were deceived by the
dim light, or by some momentary dizziness which blurred
our vision.

SGANARELLE

Oh, no, Sir! Don't try to explain away what we both so
clearly saw. Nothing could be more real than that nod of
the head, and I'm convinced that Heaven, shocked by
your behavior, wrought that miracle so as to make you see
the light, and pull you back from the brink of....

DON JUAN

Listen to me. If you pester me any further with your silly
moralizings, if you say one more word on this subject, I'll
send for a bull-whip, and have you held down by three or
four men, and give you a thousand lashes. Do you understand me?

[*Act Four • Scene One*]

SGANARELLE

Very well, Sir, very well indeed. You express yourself
most clearly. That's one of the best things about you, that
you don't in the least beat around the bush: you put
things with an admirable directness.

DON JUAN

Now then, let my dinner be served as quickly as possible.
Bring me a chair, boy!
(Ragotin brings a chair.)

SCENE TWO

LA VIOLETTE

Sir, your tailor, Monsieur Dimanche, is here, and he asks to speak with you.

SGANARELLE

Splendid; just what we needed, a visit from a creditor. What makes him think that he can come here and dun us for money, and why didn't you tell him that the master wasn't at home?

LA VIOLETTE

I've been telling him that for three quarters of an hour, but he won't believe me, and he's set himself down in there to wait.

SGANARELLE

Let him wait as long as he likes.

DON JUAN

No; on the contrary, have him come in. It's very bad policy not to be at home to one's creditors. It's only fair to give them something or other, and I know the secret of sending them away happy without paying them a penny.

SCENE THREE

DON JUAN, MONSIEUR DIMANCHE, SGANARELLE, LA VIOLETTE,
RAGOTIN

DON JUAN *(Being effusively polite.)*

Ah, Monsieur Dimanche, do come in. How delighted I
am to see you, and how annoyed I am with my servants
for not showing you in right away! I *had* given orders
that no one should be admitted; but those orders didn't
apply to you, for whom—of course—my door is always
open.

M. DIMANCHE

I'm greatly obliged to you, Sir.

DON JUAN *(Speaking to La Violette and Ragotin.)*

Confound it, you rascals, I'll teach you to keep Monsieur
Dimanche waiting in an antechamber! You must learn
how to treat important people.

M. DIMANCHE

It was nothing, Sir.

[*Act Four • Scene Three*]

DON JUAN

What! Nothing? To tell you that I wasn't at home? You, Monsieur Dimanche, my dearest friend!

M. DIMANCHE

Your servant, Sir. I came here today....

DON JUAN

Quickly now, bring a seat for Monsieur Dimanche.

M. DIMANCHE

I'm quite comfortable as I am, Sir.

DON JUAN

No, no, I insist that we sit down together.

M. DIMANCHE

That's not at all necessary.

DON JUAN

Take that stool away, and bring an armchair.

M. DIMANCHE

Sir, you must be joking. I....

DON JUAN

Not at all; I wish to give you your due, and I won't have any distinctions between us.

M. DIMANCHE

Sir....

DON JUAN

Come, have a seat.

M. DIMANCHE

There's no need of that, Sir; I only want to say one word to you. I came here....

DON JUAN

Do sit down, I beg of you.

M. DIMANCHE

No, Sir, I'm quite all right. I came here to...

DON JUAN

No, I shall not listen unless you sit down.

M. DIMANCHE

Well then, I'll do as you wish, Sir. I....

[*Act Four • Scene Three*]

DON JUAN

By Heaven, Monsieur Dimanche, you're looking well!

M. DIMANCHE

I'm well, Sir, and at your service. What brings me here....

DON JUAN

You have a fine, healthy constitution: red lips, ruddy cheeks, sparkling eyes.

M. DIMANCHE

My reason for....

DON JUAN

How is Madame Dimanche, your wife?

M. DIMANCHE

Very well, Sir, thank the Lord.

DON JUAN

She's an excellent woman.

M. DIMANCHE

She's your humble servant, Sir. I came....

DON JUAN

And your little daughter Claudine, how is she?

M. DIMANCHE

She couldn't be better.

DON JUAN

What a pretty little girl she is! I love her with all my heart.

M. DIMANCHE

You're too kind, Sir. I'd like....

DON JUAN

And little Colin, does he still make as much noise as ever with that drum of his?

M. DIMANCHE

The same as always, Sir. I....

DON JUAN

And what about your little dog Brusquet? Does he growl as fiercely as ever, and does he still gnaw the legs of all your visitors?

M. DIMANCHE

He gets worse every day, Sir; we just can't break him of the habit.

DON JUAN

Don't be surprised at my asking for news of your family; I take a great interest in them all.

M. DIMANCHE

We're infinitely obliged to you, Sir. But now....

DON JUAN *(Holding out his hand.)*

Give me the hand of friendship, Monsieur Dimanche. You *are* my friend, I hope?

M. DIMANCHE

I'm your servant, Sir.

DON JUAN

By Heaven I'm yours with all my heart.

M. DIMANCHE

You do me too much honor. I....

DON JUAN

There's nothing I wouldn't do for you.

M. DIMANCHE

Sir, your kindness is overwhelming.

DON JUAN

And there's no self-interest in it, believe me.

M. DIMANCHE

I don't deserve your gracious favor. But, Sir....

DON JUAN

Now then, Monsieur Dimanche, let's forget the formalities; will you dine with me?

M. DIMANCHE

Oh no, Sir, I must go back home at once. I....

DON JUAN *(Rising.)*

Quick, a torch to light the way for Monsieur Dimanche. And have four or five men get their muskets and escort him home.

M. DIMANCHE *(Also rising.)*

There's no need of that, Sir; I can very well get home alone. But....
> *(Sganarelle whisks the chairs away.)*

DON JUAN

Certainly not! I insist that you be escorted, for your safety concerns me deeply. I am your servant and, what's more, I am your debtor.

[*Act Four • Scene Three*]

M. DIMANCHE

Yes, Sir! That's....

DON JUAN

I make no secret of it; indeed, I tell everybody.

M. DIMANCHE

If....

DON JUAN

Would you like me to escort you home, myself?

M. DIMANCHE

Oh, Sir, you're not serious. But, Sir....

DON JUAN

Embrace me then, if you please. I beg you once again to believe that I'm wholly at your service, and that there's nothing in the world I wouldn't do for you.
(He exits.)

SGANARELLE

You must admit that my master's very devoted to you.

M. DIMANCHE

That's true; he's so gracious to me, and pays me so many compliments, that I never know how to ask him for money.

SGANARELLE

I assure you that his whole household would gladly die for you. I could almost wish that something bad would happen to you—that someone would take a notion to thrash you with a cane or club; then you'd see how zealously we all....

M. DIMANCHE

I'm sure of it; but, Sganarelle, I beg you to give him a little reminder of the money he owes me.

SGANARELLE

Oh, you mustn't worry about that! He'll pay you royally.

M. DIMANCHE

And you too, Sganarelle, you owe me something on your own account.

SGANARELLE

Tut! Don't mention it.

M. DIMANCHE

What do you mean? I....

SGANARELLE

D'you think I'm not aware of what I owe you?

M. DIMANCHE

No, but....

SGANARELLE

Come, Monsieur Dimanche, I'll light your way to the door.

M. DIMANCHE

But my money....

SGANARELLE *(Taking M. Dimanche by the arm.)*

You can't be serious.

M. DIMANCHE

I want....

SGANARELLE *(Pulling him.)*

Come.

M. DIMANCHE

I came here....

SGANARELLE *(Pushing him.)*

Tut! Tut! Don't talk of trifles!

M. DIMANCHE

But....

SGANARELLE *(Pushing him.)*

Tut, Monsieur Dimanche!

M. DIMANCHE

I....

SGANARELLE *(Pushing him offstage.)*

Tut, I tell you!

SCENE FOUR

DON LUIS, DON JUAN, LA VIOLETTE, SGANARELLE

LA VIOLETTE *(To Don Juan, who has reentered.)*

Sir, your father is here.

DON JUAN

Well, how opportune! It's just what was needed to drive
me out of my mind.

DON LUIS

I can see that I discommode you, and that you'd gladly do
without a visit from me. Each of us, in fact, is wonderfully
vexing to the other, and if you're tired of the sight of me,
I in my turn am tired of your low behavior. Alas, how
foolish men are when, instead of letting the Lord decide
what's good for them, they presume to know better than
He, and plague him with their blind desires and thought-
less entreaties! To have a son was the dearest wish of my
heart; for that I prayed unceasingly and with a matchless
fervor; and the son I got by wearying Heaven with my
pleas is the sorrow and torment of my life, rather than its
joy and consolation. Can you conceive how pained I am
by the multitude of your misdeeds, the endless stream of
scandals which I seek in vain to excuse before the world?
They have forced me, again and again, to beg the King's

indulgence, so straining his patience that the merit of my
services, and the influence of my friends, will soon be
powerless to sway him. Oh, how low you have sunk! Are
you not ashamed, to be so unworthy of your origins?
What right have you now to take pride in your birth? And
what have you done in the world that would prove you a
gentleman? Do you think that it suffices to bear the name
and the coat of arms—that we may glory in our noble
blood and at the same time wallow in infamy? No, no,
birth is nothing if virtue doesn't attend it. We share the
glory of our ancestors only in proportion as we strive to
resemble them; and their splendid deeds, which shed a
lustre upon us, oblige us to honor them in kind—to follow in their footsteps, and not to forsake their fine example if we wish to be their true descendants. It means
nothing, therefore, that you're descended from the fore-
bears who begot you: they disown you as not of their
blood, and their illustrious acts reflect no credit on you;
on the contrary, their radiance but reveals your dark dis-
honor, and their glory is a torch whereby all eyes can see
the squalor of your ways. Know, then, that a gentleman
who lives wickedly is a monster, a freak of nature, and
that virtue is our best claim to nobility. The name that a
man may sign matters less to me than the deeds he does,
and I'd think more highly of a porter's son who was a decent man than of a king's son who lived like you.

DON JUAN

Sir, if you'd take a chair, you could talk more comfortably.

DON LUIS

No, insolent wretch, I've no wish to sit down or to speak
further, and I can see that nothing I've said has touched

your heart or mind. But be aware, my unworthy son, that
your actions have strained my paternal feelings to the
breaking-point, and that I shall manage, sooner than you
think, to put a stop to your depravities, forestall the wrath
of Heaven, and by your punishment cleanse myself of the
shame of having given you life.

(He exits.)

SCENE FIVE

DON JUAN, SGANARELLE

DON JUAN

Aagh! The best thing you could do is to die as soon as possible. Every man should have his turn, and it's an outrage when fathers threaten to outlive their sons.
(*He sits down in his armchair.*)

SGANARELLE

Oh, Sir, you shouldn't....

DON JUAN

I shouldn't what?

SGANARELLE *(Quaking.)*

Well, Sir....

DON JUAN *(Rising from his chair.)*

I shouldn't what?

SGANARELLE

Sir, you shouldn't have let him say those things to you;
indeed, you should have seized him by the shoulders and
thrown him out. What could be more impertinent than
for a father to reproach his son, and bid him mend his
ways, and remember his ancestors, and lead a decent life,
and a hundred other stupidities of the kind? Why should
a man like you, who knows how to live, put up with that
sort of thing? I'm amazed by your patience; had I been in
your place, I'd have sent him packing.
(Aside.)
O damnable servility! What have you made me say?

DON JUAN

Will my dinner soon be served?

SCENE SIX

DON JUAN, DOÑA ELVIRA, RAGOTIN, SGANARELLE

RAGOTIN

Sir, there's a lady in a veil who wants to speak with you.

DON JUAN

Who could it be?

SGANARELLE

We'll soon know.

DOÑA ELVIRA *(Veiled, and wearing a species of cassock.)*

Don't be surprised, Don Juan, to see me at this hour and in this costume. The most urgent motives compel me to make this visit, and what I have to say will permit of no delay. I don't come here full of that wrath which I displayed before, and you see me much changed from what I was this morning. No longer am I that Doña Elvira who prayed for your punishment, whose angry spirit spoke nothing but threats, breathed nothing but vengeance. Heaven has purged my soul of all the unworthy passion I felt for you, all the stormy emotions of a guilty attachment, all the shameful transports of a gross and earthly love; the love for you that remains in my heart is a flame cleansed of everything sensual; a holy tenderness; a detached, disinterested love which asks nothing for itself and thinks only of your welfare.

DON JUAN *(Sotto voce to Sganarelle.)*

I do believe you're crying.

SGANARELLE

Forgive me.

DOÑA ELVIRA

It was that pure and perfect love which led me here to help you, to convey to you a warning from Heaven, and to pull you back, if possible, from the precipice toward which you are blindly rushing. Yes, Don Juan, I'm now well aware of all the excesses of your life, and the same Heaven which has touched my heart, and made me confront my errors, has inspired me to come and see you, and to tell you on its behalf that your offenses have exhausted its mercy, that its terrible wrath is ready to fall upon you, that it lies within your power to avert that wrath by a prompt repentance, and that you have, perhaps, no more than a day in which to save yourself from the worst of calamities. As for me, I am no longer tied to you by any earthly bond; I've recovered, thanks to Heaven, from all my passionate follies; I'm resolved to retire from the world, and all I ask is time enough in which to expiate my lapse, and to gain a pardon, through austere penitence, for the madness that came of my sinful infatuation. But it would greatly grieve me, in my peaceful convent, if someone I had tenderly cherished were made a dread example of the justice of Heaven; and it will be an infinite joy to me if I can persuade you to ward off the terrible blow that threatens you. Don Juan, I entreat you, as a last favor, to grant me that sweet consolation; don't refuse me your salvation, for which I ask with tears in my eyes; and if your own self-interest doesn't move you, be moved at least by my prayers, and spare me the agony of seeing you condemned to eternal torments.

SGANARELLE *(Aside.)*

Poor woman!

DOÑA ELVIRA

I loved you with the utmost tenderness; nothing in the world was so dear to me as you; I forgot my vows for you; for you, there was nothing that I would not do; and all I ask in return is that you amend your life and avoid your eternal ruin. Save yourself, I beg you, whether for your sake or for mine. Once again, Don Juan, I ask it with tears in my eyes; and if the tears of one you have loved are not enough, I beseech you by whatever is most able to touch your heart.

SGANARELLE *(Aside, looking at Don Juan.)*

His *heart!* He has the heart of a tiger.

DOÑA ELVIRA

With those words I shall leave you, having said all that I had to say.

[*Act Four • Scene Six*]

DON JUAN

Madam, it's late. Stay here: we shall make you as comfortable as we can.

DOÑA ELVIRA

No, Don Juan, don't detain me.

DON JUAN

Madam, you will give me pleasure by staying, I assure you.

DOÑA ELVIRA

No, I tell you; let's waste no time in idle talk. Let me go quickly, don't offer to see me out, and think only of profiting by my good counsel.

SCENE SEVEN

DON JUAN, SGANARELLE, LA VIOLETTE, RAGOTIN

DON JUAN

D'you know, I still have some slight feeling for her, and I
found a certain charm in that bizarre new style of hers.
Her careless dress, her languishing look, her tears stirred
up in me a few small embers of a dead fire.

SGANARELLE

In short, her words had no effect on you at all.

DON JUAN

Quick now, my dinner.

SGANARELLE

Very good, Sir.

DON JUAN *(Sitting down at the table.)*

Still, Sganarelle, we must give some thought to
reforming.

[*Act Four • Scene Seven*]

SGANARELLE

Oh, Sir! Do you mean that?

DON JUAN

Yes, indeed, we must reform; twenty or thirty more years of this sort of life, and then we'll think about it.

SGANARELLE

Oh.

DON JUAN

What do you say to that?

SGANARELLE

Nothing. Here comes your dinner.
(*Sganarelle takes a piece of food from one of the platters which are being carried in, and pops it into his mouth.*)

DON JUAN

You seem to have a swollen cheek; what's the matter? Speak up, now; what's happened to you?

SGANARELLE

Nothing

[Act Four • Scene Seven]

DON JUAN

Let me look. Good Lord, his cheek is all distended. Quick, bring me a lancet to pierce it with. The poor fellow's in dreadful shape, and that abscess might choke him. Wait.... My, what a great lump it was. Ah, you thieving rascal!

SGANARELLE

Heavens, Sir, I only wanted to make sure that your cook hadn't used too much salt, or too much pepper.

DON JUAN

Come, sit down there and eat. I'll have a task for you when I've finished with dinner. You're hungry, it seems.

SGANARELLE (Sitting down at the table.)

I should say I am! I've had nothing to eat since morning. Do have a taste of that, it couldn't be more delicious.
(Ragotin repeatedly removes Sganarelle's plate,
as soon as the latter has served anything upon it.)
My plate, my plate! Not so fast, if you please. For goodness' sake, my young friend, you're a bit too quick with the clean dishes! And you, La Violette, you know just when to pour the wine, don't you?
(While La Violette is pouring wine for Sganarelle,
Ragotin snatches his plate away again.)

DON JUAN

Who could be knocking in that manner?

[*Act Four • Scene Seven*]

SGANARELLE

Who in the devil has come disrupting our dinner-hour?

DON JUAN

I intend to dine in peace; let no one be admitted.

SGANARELLE

Leave it to me; I'll go to the door myself.

DON JUAN (*To Sganarelle, who returns looking frightened.*)

Well, what is it? What's the matter?

SGANARELLE (*Nodding his head as the Statue did.*)

The...it's there!

DON JUAN

I'll go and see; and I'll show you that nothing can frighten me.

SGANARELLE

Oh, poor Sganarelle, where can you hide?

SCENE EIGHT

DON JUAN, THE STATUE OF THE COMMANDER,
SGANARELLE, LA VIOLETTE, RAGOTIN

DON JUAN *(To La Violette and Ragotin.)*

Quick now, a chair, and set another place.
      (Don Juan and the Statue sit down at the table.
           To Sganarelle.)
Come, come, sit down with us.

SGANARELLE

Sir, I'm not hungry any more.

DON JUAN

You heard me, sit down. Bring the wine! Join me in a
toast, Sganarelle: to the Commander's health! Give him
some wine.

SGANARELLE

Sir, I'm not thirsty.

DON JUAN

Drink your wine, and sing us a song to amuse the
Commander.

[*Act Four • Scene Eight*]

SGANARELLE

I have a cold, Sir.

DON JUAN

That doesn't matter. Let's have it. And the rest of you, gather round and sing the harmony.

THE STATUE

Don Juan, that will do. I invite you to come and dine with me tomorrow. Have you the courage to accept?

DON JUAN

Yes, I shall come, accompanied only by Sganarelle.

SGANARELLE

Thank you kindly, but tomorrow is a fast day for me.

DON JUAN *(To Sganarelle.)*

Here, take this torch and light the Commander's way.

THE STATUE

There's no need for light when Heaven is our guide.

ACT FIVE

SCENE ONE

DON LUIS, DON JUAN, SGANARELLE
In the country, near the city gates.

DON LUIS

Ah, my son, can it be that Heaven, in its mercy, has heard my prayers? Is it really true, what you tell me? You wouldn't delude me, I'm sure, with a false hope....Dare I believe this miraculous change of heart?

DON JUAN *(Playing the hypocrite.)*

Yes, I've renounced all my sinful ways, and I'm not the same man whom you saw yesterday evening. Heaven has wrought in me a sudden change—a change that will astound the world: It's awakened my soul and opened my eyes, so that I look back with horror on my long blindness, and the wicked excesses of the life I've led. When I review in my mind all the abominable things I've done, it amazes me that Heaven has suffered them for so long, without sending down its just wrath upon my head. I'm thankful for the mercy it's shown in not punishing my crimes; and I mean to make good use of that forbearance, showing the world a swift amendment of my ways, atoning thereby for my scandalous past, and striving to win a full pardon from Heaven. Those things are what I undertake to do, and I beg you, Sir, to support me in that

effort, and to help me select a spiritual advisor who will
guide my steps on the path of redemption.

DON LUIS

Ah, my dear son, how readily a father's love can be restored, and how quickly a few words of repentance can
make a son's offenses vanish! I've already forgotten the
hours of anguish you've cost me; all that is erased from
my mind by the words you've just spoken. I'm beside myself with joy; these tears are tears of happiness; all my
prayers are answered, and I have nothing more to ask of
the Lord. Embrace me, my son, and don't fail, I implore
you, to persevere in your laudable intentions. As for me,
I'll go at once and bear this glad news to your mother,
share my rapturous delight with her, and render thanks to
Heaven for the holy decision it's moved you to make.

SCENE TWO

DON JUAN, SGANARELLE

SGANARELLE

Oh, Sir, how I rejoice in your conversion! I've waited a long time for this, and now, thank Heaven, my dearest wish is granted.

DON JUAN

Don't be an ass!

SGANARELLE

How am I an ass?

DON JUAN

Come, now! Did you take my words for the real thing? Did you think my lips were speaking for my heart?

SGANARELLE

What! Didn't you.... You mean.... You mean you didn't....

(Aside.)

Oh, what a man! What a man!

DON JUAN

No, no, I haven't changed at all, and my views are what
they always were.

SGANARELLE

You're not shaken, then, by the awesome mystery of a
statue that walks and talks?

DON JUAN

There is, indeed, something there that I don't under·
stand; but whatever it may be, it's not enough to sway my
mind and intimidate my soul; and if I've announced an intention to mend my ways, and embark on an exemplary
mode of life, I've done so from pure calculation and self-
interest. I said what I said as part of a scheme, a tactic, a
prudent strategy of deception which I'm forced to adopt,
in order to humor a father whose help I need, and protect
myself from all sorts of vexations that men might visit
upon me. I take you into my confidence, Sganarelle, because it pleases me that someone should know my true
feelings, and the reasons which compel me to act as I do.

SGANARELLE

What! You still don't believe in anything at all, and yet
you intend to pose as a pious, right-thinking man?

DON JUAN

Why not? There are plenty of others who play that game,
and who wear the same mask as I to deceive the world.

SGANARELLE

Oh, what a man! What a man!

DON JUAN

It's no longer shameful to be a dissembler; hypocrisy is now a fashionable vice, and all fashionable vices pass for virtues. The part of God-fearing man is the best possible role to play nowadays, and in our present society the hypocrite's profession has extraordinary advantages. It's an art whose dishonesty always goes unchallenged; even if the whole world sees through the imposture, no one dares denounce it. All the other vices of mankind are subject to censure, and anyone is free to upbraid them roundly; but hypocrisy is a privileged vice which knows how to silence every tongue and enjoy a perfect impunity. The hypocrite, by means of pious pretenses, attaches himself to the company of the devout, and anyone who then assails him is set upon by a great phalanx of the godly—wherein those who act sincerely, and have a true religious fervor, are always the dupes of the others. The true believers are easily hoodwinked by the false, and blindly second those who ape their piety. I can't tell you how many men I know who, by means of a feigned devotion, have glossed over the sins of their youth, wrapped themselves in the cloak of religion, and in that holy disguise are now free to be the worst of scoundrels! It makes no difference if their intrigues are sometimes exposed and their true natures laid bare; they don't cease, on that account, to be respected, since by soulful groans, and bowings of the head, and rollings of the eye toward Heaven, they can readily persuade the world to excuse whatever they do.

I propose to take refuge in this modish style of deception, and thus protect myself and my interests. I shan't
give up any of my cherished pursuits, but I'll be careful to
pursue them quietly and on the sly. If ever my secret life
is discovered, I won't have to lift a finger: the whole cabal
of the pious will take my side, and defend me against all
comers. In short, I've found the ideal way to do whatever
I like and go scot-free. I'll set myself up as censor of the
conduct of others, I'll condemn everybody, and I'll approve of no one but myself. If anyone offends me, however slightly, I'll never forgive him, but shall nurse instead
a secret and implacable hatred. I'll appoint myself the
Avenger of Heaven, and with that convenient pretext I'll
harass my enemies, accuse them of impiety, and stir up
against them a swarm of ignorant zealots, who'll assail
them in public, heap them with defamations, and offi-
ciously doom them to Hell. A clever man will thus exploit
men's follies, and adapt his style to the vices of the age.

SGANARELLE

Great Heavens! What do I hear you say? All that was
needed to perfect your immorality was that you become a
hypocrite, and now it's happened—you've embraced the
very worst of iniquities. Sir, this crowning horror is too
much for me, and I can't keep silent about it. Do whatever you like to me—beat me, bludgeon me, kill me if
you want to; I must nevertheless speak my mind and say
to you what, as your loyal valet, I feel bound to say. Remember, Sir, that if the pitcher goes to the well too often,
it gets broken at last; and as an author whose name I forget has memorably said, man in this world is like a bird
upon a bough; the bough is attached to the trunk; whoever's attached to the trunk has upright values; upright
values are better than fine words; fine words are what you

hear at court; the court is full of courtiers; courtiers follow the fashion; fashion derives from fancy; fancy is a faculty of the soul; the soul is what gives us life; life ends in death; death makes us think of Heaven; Heaven is above the earth; the earth is both land and sea; the sea is subject to storms; storms toss ships; a ship needs a good pilot; a good pilot has prudence; prudence is seldom found in the young; the young should obey the old; the old are fond of comfort and riches; riches make people rich; the rich aren't poor; the poor live in dire necessity; necessity has no law; whoever knows no law lives like a brute beast; and consequently you shall be condemned to dwell below with all the devils.

DON JUAN

What a fine chain of reasoning!

SGANARELLE

If you don't repent after that, so much the worse for you.

SCENE THREE

DON CARLOS

This chance encounter, Don Juan, is most opportune; I'll
be glad to discuss matters here, rather than at your lodg-
ings, and to learn from you what decisions you've made.
You'll remember that I took on, in your presence, the responsibility for settling our quarrel. As for me, it's my
frank and fervent wish that the affair be settled without
violence; I hope that I may persuade you to take the
peaceable course, and that I may see you publicly acknowledge my sister as your wife.

DON JUAN *(In a hypocritical tone of voice.)*

Alas! I wish with all my heart that I could give you the
satisfaction that you desire; but Heaven expressly forbids
me to do so. It's inspired in me a determination to lead a
better life, and I now have no other thought than to sever
all wordly attachments, cast aside all hollow vanities, and
seek henceforward, by austere disciplines, to atone for the
transgressions of my heedless youth.

DON CARLOS

Your intentions, Don Juan, don't jar with what I've pro-
posed; the companionship of a lawful wife could accord

very well with the laudable ideas that Heaven has inspired in you.

DON JUAN

Alas, it would never do, as your sister has already decided. She has retired to a convent. We both saw the light at the same moment.

DON CARLOS

Her retirement is unacceptable to us, because it might well seem the result of your scorn for her and for our family; our honor demands that she live with you.

DON JUAN

That cannot be, I assure you. For my part, I've desired that happiness more than anything in the world, and even today I asked Heaven's aid and advice in the matter; but while I was communing with Heaven, I heard a voice say that I must think no more about your sister, and that I would never find salvation if she and I lived together.

DON CARLOS

Do you expect us, Don Juan, to be impressed by these high-flown excuses?

DON JUAN

I merely obey the voice of Heaven.

[*Act Five • Scene Three*]

DON CARLOS

Am I to settle for such an unlikely story?

DON JUAN

It's Heaven's will.

DON CARLOS

You've taken my sister out of her convent, and now you
abandon her?

DON JUAN

So Heaven ordains.

DON CARLOS

And we're to swallow this insult to our honor?

DON JUAN

You must take that up with Heaven.

DON CARLOS

Heaven! Can you think of nothing but Heaven?

DON JUAN

That's what Heaven would have me do.

DON CARLOS

Enough, Don Juan; I understand you. I shan't settle accounts with you here; this is not the place for it. But I shall find you soon again.

DON JUAN

Do as you wish; you know that I don't lack courage, and that I know how to use my sword when I must. In a few minutes I shall be passing along the quiet little side-street that leads toward the great monastery. I declare to you, however, that I have no wish to fight; Heaven forbids me to harbor such a thought. But should you attack me, we'll see what happens.

DON CARLOS

We'll see. Yes, we shall see.

SCENE FOUR

DON JUAN, SGANARELLE

SGANARELLE

Sir, what's this infernal new manner you've adopted? It's the worst yet by far; and, wicked though you were, I liked you better as you used to be. I always had hopes for your salvation, but now I despair of it, and I think that Heaven, which has put up with you till now, won't tolerate this last enormity.

DON JUAN

Nonsense. Heaven isn't so fussy as you think. Why, if every time a man....
(A Spectre enters, in the form of a veiled woman.)

SGANARELLE *(Seeing the Spectre.)*

Oh, Sir, Heaven has something to say to you! It's giving you a warning.

DON JUAN

If Heaven's giving me a warning, and wants me to understand, it must speak a bit more clearly.

SCENE FIVE

DON JUAN
A SPECTRE—*in the form of a veiled woman*
SGANARELLE

THE SPECTRE

Don Juan has only a moment left in which to avail himself of Heaven's mercy. If he does not repent at once, he is doomed to perdition.

SGANARELLE

Do you hear that, Sir?

DON JUAN

Who dares address me so? I think I recognize that voice.

SGANARELLE

It's a ghost, Sir! I can tell by its way of walking.

DON JUAN

Ghost, or shadow, or devil—whatever it is—I mean to have a look at it.
> (*The Spectre changes shape, and now represents
> Time with his scythe in hand.*)

[*Act Five · Scene Five*]

SGANARELLE

Oh, Heavens! Do you see, Sir, how it's changed its shape?

DON JUAN

Hah! Nothing on earth can terrify me, and I mean to find out, with my sword, whether this thing is body or spirit.
  (The Spectre vanishes before Don Juan can strike it.)

SGANARELLE

Oh, Sir! After so many signs and warnings, you must give in and hasten to repent.

DON JUAN

No, no. Whatever may happen, it won't be said of me that I stooped to repentance. Come, follow me.

SCENE SIX

THE STATUE, DON JUAN, SGANARELLE

THE STATUE

Stay, Don Juan! You promised yesterday to come and
dine with me.

DON JUAN

Yes. Where are we to go?

THE STATUE

Give me your hand.

DON JUAN

Here it is.

THE STATUE

Obstinacy in sin, Don Juan, leads to a terrible death.
Those who refuse the mercy of Heaven invite its
thunderbolts.

DON JUAN

O God, what's this I feel? An invisible fire consumes me; I can't bear any more of this; my whole body's become a blazing furnace. Oh...!

(Thunder and lightning descend upon Don Juan, with great noise and bright flashes. The earth opens and swallows him up, and great flames rise out of the pit into which he has fallen.)

SGANARELLE

Oh! My back wages! What about my wages? My master's death gives satisfaction to everyone: the Heaven he offended, the girls he ruined, the families he dishonored, the laws he broke, the parents he outraged, the wives he led astray, the husbands he drove to despair—they're all well pleased. I'm the only one who's unhappy. Alas, my wages! My wages! Who'll pay me my wages?